C H Spurgeon

D1322110

C H SPURGEON ON CREATION AND EVOLUTION

An interview conducted by David Harding

Day.One

ISBN 1-84625-021-8

9 781846 250217 >

British Library Cataloguing in Publication Data available

Published by Day One Publications
Ryelands Road, Leominster, HR6 8NZ
Telephone 01568 613 740   FAX 01568 611 473

email—sales@dayone.co.uk
web site—www.dayone.co.uk

Designed by Steve Devane and printed by Gutenberg Press, Malta.

In memory of
Professor Verna Wright M.D., F.R.C.P.

A great man of science
A great man of God

May this be a further contribution in leading us,
in his own catchphrase,
'On to victory!'

Contents

COMMENDATIONS

In 1854, twenty-year-old Charles Haddon Spurgeon was called to the London church he would pastor for the rest of his life. Five years later, Charles Darwin published his magnum opus, *On the Origin of Species*. Spurgeon was an outspoken critic of the evolutionary hypothesis from the very start—one of the first Christian leaders to recognize the grave spiritual danger posed by Darwinism. Spurgeon knew it was sheer folly to reject the revealed and unchanging truth of Scripture in favour of the vacillating theories of human rationalism. He sounded the alarm with clarity, passion, and great force.

David Harding has gleaned hundreds of Spurgeon's comments about evolution, modernism, humanism, and the follies of 'scientific' scepticism. He has edited them and arranged them brilliantly in interview format to give us a lucid, forceful, definitive, biblical answer to the theory of evolution in Spurgeon's own words. *An Interview with C H Spurgeon* is invaluable for both its historic significance and its timeless insight. I'm delighted to see this book in print.

Phil Johnson, Executive Director, Grace to you, California

All of us are surrounded by people who believe in the theory of evolution and who dismiss what the Bible teaches about creation. How can we talk to them—wisely, kindly, robustly, convincingly? This unique book will help us all. In it David Harding shows us why we should take the Bible at face value, and then conducts a series of gripping 'interviews' with the great gospel preacher, C.H. Spurgeon (1834–1892). These are enjoyable to read and are filled with helpful insights, providing us with a model of how to talk about the whole range of subjects connected with evolution. I would like to see this book on every Christian's bookshelf.

Stuart Olyott, Pastoral Director of the Evangelical Movement of Wales

Foreword

I have known Pastor David Harding of Milnrow Evangelical Church for thirty-one years. Recently he has put together a masterful piece of writing where he 'interviews' Charles Haddon Spurgeon on the vital subject of creation. With an originality similar to Spurgeon's own, David has brought out Spurgeon's stand on this crucial area of doctrine. For forty years in the latter part of the nineteenth century, this prince of preachers had immense influence, first in Waterbeach, Cambridgeshire, and then New Park Street and Metropolitan Tabernacle in London where he powerfully preached the great gospel of Christ, the Holy Spirit through him converting thousands to true faith. At Metropolitan Tabernacle alone over 14,500 people were baptised and brought into membership. The church held 6,000 people and was generally packed each Sunday for thirty years. Through his kind influence many other ministries began, most notably the East London Tabernacle under the equally blessed leadership of Archibald Brown, the Stockwell Orphanages, the Colportage Association, and the remarkable book ministry. Spurgeon's sermons and writings continue to live on today not only because of his godliness, but because of a vital principle we can all learn from—a homely style and warm use of parable, humour and picture language. Some of this shines through in Pastor Harding's own interviews with Spurgeon, and one can imagine sitting down

with the godly man in the pastor's study in London and smiling at
the keen wit of his brilliant mind!

David Livingstone once asked Spurgeon, 'How do you manage to
do two men's work in a single day?' Referring to the Holy Spirit
working in him, Spurgeon replied: 'You have forgotten that there are
two of us.' Spurgeon's influence was undoubtedly so great because as
his first priorities he was passionate about the gospel, filled with the
Spirit, and delighted in the Word of God. Spurgeon said of the
puritan John Bunyan that if one pricked him anywhere, his blood
was 'Bibline'. This was no less true of Spurgeon himself, especially in
his deep concern for the influence of evolutionary doctrine which he

opposed strongly because of his love for Scripture. Pastor Harding brings out this strong concern for the glory of God which was Spurgeon's dynamic in the controversies which marked his life. It was his underlying concern over the so-called downgrade controversy where he stood against the liberalism of the day. In Arnold Dallimore's biography of Spurgeon, which has been a blessing to so many, we read how Spurgeon loved beauty so much that he could be on a walk with a friend, and then noticing some delight in the countryside, turn to his companion and immediately suggest praying and thanking the Lord. He knew that creation, though badly marred by the curse following the fall of man, nevertheless reflected the glory of God. He had no time for evolutionary thinking and knew that it must be opposed because it undermined the authority of Scripture and removed the foundational teaching of sin and death. Pastor Harding boldly underlines Spurgeon's powerful stand on this issue, and shows that we as believers must similarly stand four square on the Scripture. It has been noteworthy that wherever revival has taken place it is always associated with a firm belief in the infallibility and plenary inspiration of Scripture. Pastor Harding shows that if we wish to have the blessing that Spurgeon had, then at the very least we must stand firmly on creation against evolutionary compromise.

In Spurgeon's day, though there was some knowledge of rocks and fossils which bore testimony to the Flood, scientific discoveries were mainly still in their infancy. Yet Spurgeon stood solidly for the biblical position, knowing that as time went on the facts of science (as against philosophies imposed upon it) would verify his position. Today there is no excuse! In all branches of science the testimony of the facts of science brings an even stronger apologetic for creation—

the wonders of digital programming of DNA, and the intricacies of micromachinery in all aspects of the animal world show the truth of Psalm 139:14, 'I will praise thee; for I am fearfully and wonderfully made.' The findings of fossils all over the world bear enormous testimony to God's judgement at the Flood, and the warning that there is a judgement we must all face in the future. In the age of the great scientists Maxwell and Faraday (both of whom were also Christians), Spurgeon stood faithfully to Scripture, and challenged the church of his day to preach a Scripture-first approach to all areas of life including science. He knew that 'since the creation of the world his invisible attributes are clearly seen, being understood by the things that are made, even his eternal power and Godhead; so that they are without excuse' (Rom. 1:20). We somehow think today that we know better. How foolish we are and how much Spurgeon would chide us, rebuke us and weep with us, for we will never know revival in the twenty-first century unless we as a church repent of evolutionary thinking—a terrible modern form of the downgrade of Scripture.

Professor Andy C. McIntosh
DSc, FIMA, C.Math, FEI, C.Eng, FInstP, MIGEM, FRAeS
Professor of Thermodynamics and Combustion Theory, Energy and Resources Research Institute, School of Process, Environmental and Materials Engineering, University of Leeds.
Author of *Genesis for Today,* Day One, Epsom, Surrey, ISBN 1 903087 15-5, 2nd Edition, 2001.

Introduction

These are accurately recorded notes of interviews, conducted by David Harding, with Mr Charles Haddon Spurgeon by means of one of the marvels of modern science, namely, a computer. In each of them a further dimension of Mr Spurgeon's antipathy to the modern theory of origins is explored.

Spurgeon, born at Kelvedon, Essex in 1834, was converted and baptised at the age of sixteen and began preaching soon after. His London ministry began at the New Park Street Chapel at the age of nineteen. The Metropolitan Tabernacle was built for him, opening in 1861. His ministry ended with his death in 1892 at the age of fifty-eight. More information about his life can be found in *Travel with C.H. Spurgeon* by Clive Anderson (Day One).

Charles Darwin's book, published in 1859, and known by the shortened title *The Origin of Species* or simply *Origin*, was at best a hypothesis. It made bold statements about the origin and development of life. Darwin's ideas were not new. Similar ideas can be traced back to Greek philosophy, but his grandfather, Erasmus Darwin (1731–1802), spawned the ideas which influenced Charles's thinking. Nevertheless, *Origin* was the first work to gain widespread publicity. It was seized on by atheists to develop evolutionary concepts, despite its flawed scientific basis, and was used to repudiate the biblical account of creation. Some leading evangelicals have yielded to the pressure to make the Bible fit Darwinism, despite Darwin himself viewing his theory as unsubstantiated by the evidence available. Spurgeon's preaching and correspondence is littered with relevant comments opposing the theory.

Spurgeon was, in some ways, a man of his day. He interpreted Genesis 1 literally, and yet he felt that this approach permitted a unique form of what is sometimes called the 'gap theory'. This may shock Spurgeon's admirers, but it would be dishonest to proceed as if he held to a 6,000–year-old creation. He considered that the planet earth was alone in the universe (if I understand all his references) at first. It was created (he seems to say) in a chaotic and unformed state for what *may have been* the equivalent of millions of years of time. The Appendix explores his attitude to the possibility of his having misunderstood the Scriptures. I consider any version of gap theory to be contrary to a correct exegesis of Genesis 1, taking into account references within Genesis and elsewhere to all that was accomplished 'in the beginning' or 'in six days'. I sincerely hope that Spurgeon's replies convey the honest and humble spirit he had about any matter on which he may have erred.

Two things emerge from the Appendix. First, that Spurgeon held to the inerrancy and authority of the whole Bible. Secondly, he is no ally to those in our day who believe that evolution was the process that brought about a species from which God chose a pair and breathed into them the image of God. Spurgeon places creation week in the recent past. He commends Mr Hely Smith for justifying the biblical account when he refutes various claims and fabrications by evolutionary scientists that originally dated certain pottery at 18,000 years old.

I adjusted Spurgeon's original statements for two reasons. The first is brevity. The original manuscript was over 50,000 words. Spurgeon repeated himself with poetic, Victorian verbosity! Secondly, some phrases and words have been adjusted to make it agreeable to the modern ear or to clarify the sense for an interview style. Nothing is out of context. Spurgeon was unambiguous in preaching. If anything is out of context, he will one day inform me. I shall anticipate that interview with joy.

Those who quote Spurgeon as the prince of preachers, and honour him in other areas, can see what kind of man he was in this vital and foundational area of the Christian faith. How can they profess admiration of him and yet be dismissive (or even derisive) of his evangelical descendants who have even more reason to take the same, and even more consistently scriptural stand? I prepared these interviews to assist my friends in creation science ministries in their support of the churches in the battle with evolution and its mongrel offspring, theistic evolution.

Spurgeon stood virtually alone with his hand on the Bible. Even his errors of understanding arose within a conviction of the inerrancy, infallibility, sufficiency and perspicuity of Holy Scripture. He had no creation science movement showing those evidences that we are privileged to review. He was certain that the Bible is self-interpreting, needing no external verification. This should be sufficient for every believer. Spurgeon states that, as we should expect, the discoverable facts in the universe can only, and will always, confirm the infallible statements in the Word. Scientific evidence supporting the historical data of Genesis 1–11 is increasingly available to us. There is, as Spurgeon also clearly stated there would be, an ongoing lack of any supporting evidence for evolution, especially any missing link, on which Darwin staked the whole of his hypothesis. There are also mountains of scientific facts flatly contradicting the evolutionary scheme or fundamental sections of it.

Some, may, by some mental gymnastics, be able to square the circle through theistic evolution, but Spurgeon laughed in the face of evolution. In his own words, 'I do not hesitate to say that the whole theory of evolution is more monstrously false and foolish than any other ever conceived beneath high heaven. It is a marvellous thing that men should be able to squeeze their minds into the belief of an absurdity which, in time to come, will be ridiculed to children in the schoolroom as an instance of the credulity of their ancestors.'

What will those who have moulded their theology do when Darwinism is debunked? Some scientists have already moved from gradualism to 'punctuated equilibrium', and left those who have altered their theology stuck with concepts that some atheistic evolutionists have difficulty with. These theologians, and their reputations, may flounder when the 'theory' arising from the voyage of the Beagle finally sinks without trace. They have built doctrinal structures on faulty foundations. It appears that only their theological inconsistencies have allowed them to build the remainder of their theology in a more evangelical way. It is sad that they did not treat the early chapters of Genesis with the same care.

I now leave you with the interviews, conducted with the aid of modern technology and its wondrous ability to search vast amounts of text on given topics in a relatively short space of time.

Spurgeon's thoughts on creation and evolution

Mr Spurgeon, I note from a cartoon mocking you, [reproduced here], that you appear to have a well-known and strongly held disbelief in the theory of evolution.

CHS I have read a good deal on the subject, and have never yet seen a fact, or the tail of a fact, which indicated the rise of one species of animal into another. The theory has been laid down, and facts fished up to support it. I believe it to be a monstrous error in philosophy, which will be a theme for ridicule before long.[1] In theology, its influence would be deadly, and this is all I care about. On the scientific matter, you do well to use your own judgement.[2]

What were your conclusions as you read and thought through the issue?

CHS Philosophically the dogma of evolution is a dream, a theory without a vestige of proof. Eventually, when children in school read of extraordinary popular delusions, this will be mentioned as one of the most absurd of them. Many a joke will be told about the follies of science in the nineteenth century. However, this is no laughing matter, because it is not only deceptive, but threatens to create a lot of trouble. There is not an ounce of truth in it. The evolution theory is in direct opposition to scriptural truth. If God's Word is true, evolution is a lie. I will not mince the matter: this is not the time for soft speaking.

What will you say to those who accuse you of being unscientific, or against any thought of progress?

CHS I am unscientific, then, and I delight to be unscientific. And if deep thinkers say this is inconsistent with progress! Well, let it be inconsistent with progress. If the whole world is against us, so much the worse for the world. Let it deny the truth if it will. That was a grand spirit of Athanasius when he said, 'Athanasius against the whole world.' And every Christian ought to be of this spirit. Is the Bible true? Then what does it matter even if every fool says that it is a lie! Hold on to it. If the Holy Spirit has taught you to trust in Christ, then trust in Christ, whatever other people do. [3]

But, we are not exactly in the majority are we?

CHS What? Do you count heads, and then jump with the larger number? Is that your way? Why, surely such a man as that is hardly worth saving. Is he a man, or is he not a cat that must look before he jumps? No, if you are a man, and you believe in Christ, stand up for Christ.4

Do you not agree, though, that the world is making progress in science and civilization in these days? It is certainly what both our scientists and politicians think.

CHS The world gets more civilized—well, I am told so, though, when I read the newspapers, I am not quite sure of it. The world gets more intelligent—I am told so, though, when I read various magazines I am not certain that it is so, for ignorance among learned and scientific men, in their discoveries, seems to make them wander further and further, not only from that which is revealed and infallible, but also from that which is rational and truthful.5

Let's move on. What do you see as the reason for evolutionary theory?

CHS Recent science has *merely* minted new apologies for scepticism. But the tree of life hasn't fossilized; it yields leaves and fruits as healing and nutritious as ever it did.6

But you are not against education, are you? After all, there seems to be an insatiable appetite in man in general to learn, enquire and search out answers about origins.

CHS I agree! It is said, 'We require food for our intellect; a man needs to develop his intellectual faculties, he needs to learn that which will enlarge and expand his mind.' Certainly, by every legitimate means. But, you needn't depart from Christ to get this, for the science of Christ crucified is the most excellent, comprehensive and sublime of all the sciences. And it is the only infallible science. Also, by all true science you will find Christ honoured, and not dishonoured, and your learning, if it is true learning, will not make you leave Christ, but lead you to see more of his creating and ruling wisdom.[7]

But, do you not think that advances in science or the study of the topic can at least help us in our search for God?

CHS Before I knew the gospel I gathered up all kinds of knowledge from here, there, and everywhere; a bit of chemistry, a bit of botany, and a bit of astronomy, and a bit of this, that, and the other. I put them altogether, in one untidy heap. When I learned the gospel, I got a shelf in my head to put everything away just where it should be. It seemed to me that, when I had discovered Christ and him crucified, I had got the centre of the system, so that I could see every other science revolving around in order. From the earth, you know, the planets appear to move in a very irregular manner—they are progressive, retrograde, stationary; but if you could stand on the sun, you would see them marching round in their constant, uniform, circular motion. So with knowledge, begin with any other science, and truth will seem to be skewed. Begin with the science of Christ crucified, and you will see every other science moving round it in complete harmony.[8]

Yes, knowing Christ as Lord and Saviour makes sense of every other compartment of knowledge. If I recall rightly, Agur, who wrote one chapter of the Bible, was a scientist in his day. Does he tell us how he viewed the issue of seeking after God?

CHS Agur was a naturalist. Proverbs 30 is saturated with allusions to natural history. He was an instructed scientist, but he felt that he could not by searching find out God, nor fashion an idea of him from his own thoughts. When he heard of the great discoveries of those who judged themselves to be superior persons, he disowned such wisdom as theirs. Other men might fish up pearls of truth from the sea; as for himself, he knew nothing except what he found in God's Word. He was content with revelation and felt that 'every word of God is pure'. All that he knew, he had been taught by God's Book. He had in thought climbed to heaven and come down again. He had listened to the speech of winds, and waves, and mountains, but he affirmed that in all this he had not discovered what he knew about God. It had come through the Lord's own Word, and he wisely gave this caution to those who thought themselves too clever for the Bible, 'Do not add to his words, Lest he rebuke you, and you be found a liar' (Proverbs 30:6). Philosophy had failed him. He went to God himself and learned from him at first hand, through his revealed wisdom.[9]

So, we begin with faith in Christ, based on the Bible alone. From there the world makes sense. This implies that the Bible is sufficient in itself. Do you really believe it, even in dealing with the evolutionary hypothesis?

CHS This Book is clear enough of itself, and this gospel is mighty enough of itself, without the aid of human wisdom. It will only be clouded, by mixing it with evolution. The river of the gospel will force its own way despite modern thought: it will win and conquer, whoever may oppose.[10]

You obviously see it mainly, even solely, as a matter of trust in God's Word. Is it really that simple?

CHS The apostle tells us, 'By faith we understand that the worlds were framed by the Word of God' (Hebrews 11:3). I know absolutely that the worlds were made by God. I am sure of it; and yet I did not see him making them. I did not see him when the light came just because he said, 'Let there be light' (Genesis 1:3), but I am quite sure that he did it. All the evolutionists in the world cannot shake my conviction that the universe was made by God.[11]

Just a minute, do you mean light was created before the sun existed?

CHS Light was created on the first day, not on the third, fourth, or sixth, but on the first day.[12]

I need to press the point, but do you really mean light without the sun?

CHS The light which broke in upon the primeval darkness was not according to ordinary laws, for as yet neither sun nor moon had been set as lights in the firmament.[13]

Is it so important to take the meaning in this way?

CHS The Lord spent a whole day in creating and arranging it—a whole day out of six. This shows that he attaches great importance to it.[14]

Point taken! Did it all really appear instantaneously though?

CHS Creation is necessarily a work which happens in an instant, for a thing either exists or not. There is the sharpest conceivable line between that which is not and that which is.[15]

But could it not mean something else? Some people think each day refers to an era, or even that the whole description is poetic, and so is subject to poetic liberties of description.

CHS How very particular God is about the time of creation! 'The evening and the morning were the first day' (Genesis 1:5). 'God said, "Let there be light," and months afterwards there came a little grey dawning, and a solitary star.' Oh no, you say, you are quoting from imagination! I am. The Scripture has it, 'God said, "Let there be light"; and there was light.' Immediate work is God's method of creating. All through the six days' work he spoke and it was done, he commanded and it stood fast.[16]

Do you not sometimes feel discouraged by the thought that the mongrel offspring of atheistic evolution, that is, theistic evolution, will become the accepted norm, even in evangelical churches?

CHS The enemies may do what they like; and preach what they please; they may take away one pulpit after another from the orthodox; they may bury us under the rubbish of evolution, and false philosophy; but we shall rise again. There may not remain one single sound expounder of the gospel; but as long as God lives, the gospel will not die. Its power may sleep, but before long it shall awake. As long as we have one match left we can set the world on fire. As long as one Bible remains the empire of Satan is in danger.[17]

Before there is such a hoped-for recovery, things may get much worse. I find the thought quite depressing.

CHS With regard to the prospect before us I may be supposed to be a prophet of evil, but I am not. I mourn the terrible defections from the truth which are now too numerous to be thought of in detail; nevertheless, I am not disquieted, much less dispirited. That cloud will blow over, as many others have done. I think the outlook is better than it was. We are not quite so afraid of that particular form of devilry which is raging now, because we begin to perceive its shape. While it was unknown it appeared to be terrible, but no more. At the first, this 'modern thought' looked very like a lion; its roaring was terrible. On closer inspection, the huge king of beasts looked more like a fox, and now we should honour it if we likened it to a wild cat. Scientific religion is empty talk without either science or religion in it. The mountain has brought forth its mouse, or, at any rate, the grand event is near. Very soon, 'advanced thought' will only be mentioned by servant girls and young Independent ministers. It has gradually declined till it may now be carried off with the slops. There is nothing in the whole bag of tricks. At this hour, I see the tide turning—not that I care much for that, for the rock on which I build is unaffected by ebb, or flood of human philosophy. Young men, who have tried modern doubt, have seen their congregations dwindle away beneath its withering power; and they are, therefore, not quite so enamoured of it as they were. It is time they should make a change, for Christian people have observed that these advanced men have not been remarkable for abundant grace, and they have even been led to think that their loose views on doctrine were all of a piece with looseness as to religion in general. Lack of soundness in the faith is usually caused by lack of conversion. Had certain men felt the power of the gospel in their own souls, they would not so readily forsake it to run after fables.[18]

It is encouraging that a good number of pastors and preachers today have rejected the theistic evolutionists' understanding of the first eleven chapters of Genesis.

CHS True, but others are wickedly prudent, and judge that certain truths which are evidently *in* God's Word had better be kept back. They say we must prophesy smooth things. To talk about the punishment of sin, to speak of eternal punishment, why, these are unpalatable. It may be that they are taught in the Word of God, but they do not suit our generation. We must pare them down. I will have no share in this. Will you? Our enlightened age says it has discovered certain things not taught in the Bible. Evolution may be clean contrary to the teaching of Genesis, but they don't care. It seems the great ambition of the age is to be original at any cost.[19]

You don't seem to have much respect for those who adjust their religion to match the spirit of the age.

CHS Guided by the principle of being 'user friendly', all religion is being toned down. Spiritual religion is despised, and an acceptable morality is set up in its place. Dress up on Sunday; behave yourself; and above all, believe everything except what you read in the Bible, and you will be all right. Be fashionable, and agree with those who profess to be scientific—this is the first and great commandment of modern men, and the second is like it—do not be different, but be as worldly as your neighbours.[20]

That is certainly a problem with Christianity in our generation, but for some reason Christians who integrate evolution and the Bible, want change and yet retain a respectful link with historic Christianity!

CHS Yes! Hear them talk—'The Apostles, the Fathers, the Puritans, they were excellent men, no doubt, but then, you see, they lived before the rise of those wonderful scientific men who have enlightened us so much.' Let me repeat what I have said: neither nineteen centuries, nor nineteen thousand centuries, can make the slightest difference to truth.[21]

Is it really so important that we emphasize these and other related truths in our preaching so precisely? Can't we simply ignore controversial issues?

CHS To a great degree I attribute the looseness of the age to the laxity of doctrine preached by its teachers. From the pulpit they have taught the people that sin is insignificant. These traitors to God and to his Christ have taught the people that there is no hell to be feared. A little, little hell, perhaps, there may be, but just punishment for sin is ignored. The precious atoning sacrifice of Christ has been derided and misrepresented by those who promised to preach it. They have given the people the name of the gospel, but the gospel itself has evaporated in their hands. From hundreds of pulpits the gospel is as dead as the dodo, and yet the preachers still take the position and name of Christ's ministers.[22]

That is a tragedy. But, what do you think is behind Darwin's popularity?

CHS The philosophy now in vogue labours to shut God out of his creation. They inform us that by some means this world evolved. They won't be content with it for long. They don't care about evolution, except that it serves their purpose of escaping from the thought of God. If by some means or other vain men could create a world without a God, they would be delighted; and that philosopher who comes nearest to the invention of a subtle lie, which justifies their forgetfulness of God, is the prince of the hour.[23]

But, surely, it cannot be the case that Christians have accepted the theory because of a desire to shut God out. What can their reason be?

CHS How many have forsaken the simple gospel, and turned away from the belief in their Bible which their mother had, and in which their father died, because they want to be considered very thoughtful, clever and superior people! Now, whenever a person gives up his belief in the Word of God because it requires that he should believe a good deal, his unbelief requires him to believe a great deal more. Whatever difficulties there are in the faith of Christ, they are not one-tenth as great as the absurdities in any system of unbelief which seeks to take its place. I say without hesitation that the whole doctrine of evolution, which fascinates men today, is ten thousand times more absurd than the most ridiculous travesty of what is taught in the Word of God, and that it requires more faith, and far greater gullibility than to believe any doctrine which is deduced from Holy Scripture.[24]

What reasons, other than a desire to be thought clever, might be behind this loss of confidence in the historicity of Genesis 1–11?

CHS Often the less a man knows of the inner life, and the less he cares to speak of it, the more heartily he is in favour of new theology, the theory of evolution, and the condemnation of all settled doctrine.[25]

I realize that the Bible teaches that there is a moral cause for not coming to Christ and also for apostasy from Christ. Do you think this may also be why so many reject these chapters of Genesis as an account of history?

CHS The objections, which those who object to the Lord mention, are not their real objections. Their pretended difficulties are red herrings, to turn the scent from their real reasons. Many quibble with Christ because they do not want to give up their sin. They pick up some technical question, some difficulty raised by geology or evolution, or something or other, and they make a fuss over it, while the real impediment is that they are living an unclean life, and do not want to give up their evil ways. But they do not care to mention the real difficulty, and therefore they pretend they have another problem. The sincere seeker does not play at pretend problems, but speaks out at once and says what the point is really hindering him.[26]

What you are describing is sheer hypocrisy, isn't it?

CHS Perhaps it was left for this age to see the growth of the vilest hypocrisy that ever appeared among the sons of men. We have had abundant proof that the most scientifically minded men, who have been to the seventh heaven of wisdom, have nevertheless proved that they could not receive the things of the kingdom of God, by their determined opposition and enmity against anything like the truth as it is in Jesus. When you hear them blaspheming the holy name of Christ, or bringing what they call 'scientific facts' against the truth of revelation, don't be amazed as though it were some new thing, but write this down in your memorandum book—the Holy Spirit said of old, 'The natural man does not receive the things of the Spirit of God' (1 Corinthians 2:14), and these men live to prove that what the Spirit of God said was exactly true.[27]

Don't you find it all confusing to be having so much so-called evidence against the Bible and other opposition to the gospel of the Lord Jesus?

CHS The unbelieving world is labouring to create confusion. The higher critics, the scientific discoverers, the cultured, and all the other boasters of this enlightened century are up in arms against those who believe in Jesus. When I think of how this century has been befooled by its statesmen and philosophers, I, for one, feel small reverence for it. Perhaps it has the most light, but it doesn't have the best eyes. Well, let all this 'wisdom' of the world assail us! Let proud hypocrites point their finger and say, 'You trust in Christ; you rely upon Jesus of Nazareth alone for your salvation; you are old-fashioned, and as much out of place as the extinct animals would be if they could come back again.' I affirm that if all the wise men in the world concentrated all their scorn into one universal sneer of contempt, I do not think it would affect me the turn of a hair.[28]

What do you think of the suggestion that evolution makes more sense to an educated mind than a literal six-day creation?

CHS The man who thinks so has given up the old doctrine because it was difficult, and has accepted a new one, which is ten times more difficult. He did not want to be gullible, and now he is a hundred times more so. Creation staggered him, so he tries to believe in evolution. Faith in Jesus seemed hard, but he must now accept agnosticism. The difficulties of unbelief are ten times greater than the difficulties of faith.[29]

Do you really think that those who reject creation to accept an evolutionary worldview are really gullible? That is quite a revolutionary thought.

CHS The most gullible persons in the world are unbelievers. It takes ten thousand times more faith to be an unbeliever than to be a believer in revelation. They say I am gullible, because I believe in a great First Cause who created the heavens and the earth, and that God became man and died for sin. I tell him I may be very gullible, as he conceives it, but what I believe is perfectly consistent with my reason. 'But,' he says, 'I am not at all gullible.' 'Sir,' I say, 'I ask you one thing. Do you think this Bible exists without being made? If you should say I am gullible because I believe it had a printer and a binder, I should say you were infinitely more gullible, if you assure me that it was not made at all. And when you begin to tell me your theories about creation—that atoms floated through space, and came to a certain shape, I should resign the palm of gullibility to you. You also believe that man came to exist through the improvement of other creatures. I have read that you say, that simple organisms improved themselves until they came to be microscopic organisms—that afterwards they grew into fishes— that fishes wanted to fly, and wings grew—after that they wanted to crawl, and legs came, and by divers steps they became monkeys, and then monkeys became men, and you believe yourself to be second cousin to an orang-utan. Now, I may be very gullible, but really not so gullible as you are. I may believe very strange things. I may believe that the earth was drowned with water, and many other strange things, as you call them; but as for your creed, it as much exceeds mine in gullibility (if I am gullible), as an ocean does a drop.' It requires the hardest faith in the world to deny the Scriptures, because the man, in his inner heart, knows they are true. Wherever he goes, something whispers to him, 'You may be wrong—perhaps you are,' and it is as much as he can do to say, 'Lie down, conscience! Down with you. I must not let you speak, or I could not deliver my lecture tomorrow, I could not be with my friends, I could not go to such-and-such a club; for I cannot afford to keep a conscience, if I cannot afford to keep a God.'[30]

But is there no case for thinking the universe may have just happened?

CHS If I were to assert that this Metropolitan Tabernacle grew up by chance, without either architect or builder, I should be a liar as well as a fool; but I should have just as much reason to say that as to declare that the universe came into existence without the formal command of the great Creator. Men who deny the plain teaching of Scripture on this point are indeed fools.[31]

What should our response be, then, to those who are tempted to give intellectual credibility to evolution and mix it into their understanding of the Bible?

CHS The present idols of the mind are just as worthless as those of former times. The god of modern thought is a monkey. If those who believed in evolution said their prayers rightly, they would begin them with, 'Our Father, which art up a tree.' Did they not all come from a monkey, according to their own statement? They came by 'development', from the basest of material, and they do not misrepresent their origin! If you are not acquainted with this new gospel, I would not advise you to become acquainted with it; it is a sheer waste of time to know anything about it at all. Modern men are able to believe anything except their Bibles. They will believe anything, so long as it is not in the Scriptures; but if it is founded on Scripture, they are, of course, prepared to doubt and quibble and find fault straight away. The credulity of the new theologians is as amazing as their scepticism. But we shall see the monkey-god go down yet, and evolution will be ridiculed as it deserves to be. This philosophy, whose aim is to get rid of God, has nothing to support it in fact or nature. It will fly as chaff before the wind, and eventually[32] nobody will admit that he even thought of believing it. The new religion will be regarded as a craze, an emanation from a madhouse; and every man will be ashamed to think that he stopped to hear or read anything about it. So idiotic is it from beginning to end, that it will become a standing joke for ages to come. The whole of this thing, which has been so cunningly and carefully devised to dethrone God, and cast down his gospel, will be held in derision.[33]

Couldn't it be argued that, combining creation with evolution is actually the way forward? Christianity might retain its credibility that way, and show that the church isn't in the Dark Ages? This is what modern theologians impress on some of us.

CHS Their road is both new and broad. What! Were the saints of former ages all mistaken? The martyrs—did they die for a falsehood, and shed their blood for doctrines which criticism explodes? The men of whom the world was not worthy, were they all deceived by theories which time has disproved? Did nobody know anything till Darwin appeared? Were those who believed that 'the things which are seen were not made of things which do appear' (Hebrews 11:3) complete fools? Is it quite so certain as some think it, that the things which were made grew out of things already existing? Of course, I know that nowadays men are so wonderfully intelligent that they have discovered that human life has 'evolved' from lower life. We are the heirs of oysters,[34] and the close relatives of apes. It has taken considerable time to complete the evolution; and yet we still meet with some very hard shells, and some men are not much above animals—especially such men as can be duped by this hypothesis! Were the old-fashioned believers all wrong? No, they were not wrong: their lives and their deaths prove that they were right. We shall be wrong if we leave the old and tried paths for these new roads which lead into fathomless bogs of unbelief.[35]

What will happen to the modern theology if, or rather, when evolution loses its charm to atheists?

CHS It may happen that, in a little time, evolution will be the standing joke of schoolboys. The same is true of modern divinity which bows its knee in blind idolatry of so-called science. Now I say with all my heart, that the gospel which I preached forty years ago I will still preach in forty years time if I am alive.[36]

I have heard that in some theological colleges new interpretations of origins rise up and are preached with certainty only because some well-known scientist has thrown doubt upon the Bible account.

CHS I have seen and heard the like. We are told, 'Well, he is very educated; a Fellow of Brazenface College, and has written a book upsetting the old teachings.' If an educated man writes any nonsense, of course it will have a hearing. There is no opinion so insane but, if it has the patronage of so-called scientific men, it will be believed in certain quarters. I have tried to get what I could out of the books of those who labour in new theologies, but I have been struck with the remarkably poor results of their pretentious writings.[37]

Isn't it a tragedy when Bible colleges seem more focussed on theories undermining the Bible than declaring the truths so plainly asserted in its text? The wonder of it is that these colleges and their lecturers think they have found the key to interpreting the Bible—new light shining on a new path. They think those who stick with historic Christianity, are living in the ignorance of a former generation.

CHS Every now and then a scientific gentleman picks up a flint arrow-head, and he strikes a wonderful light with it; and he that has a tinder-box ready and a brimstone match may soon think he has got the true light, till another philosopher comes and, with the lid of the same tinder-box, puts out that light. This is the cardinal virtue of philosophers; they extinguish one another! Their fine-spun theories do not often survive the fleeting generation that admires them. Then fresh theories of unbelief come, which live their day, like ephemera,[38] and then expire. Not so the light of Christ; it burns on, and beams forever.[39]

The grief is when one's Christian friends waver or fall, and become persuaded by the false theories underpinning science today.

CHS I have friends, too, who have been dazed by the light of 'public opinion'—which is a very bright light. And I have known some decent scholars who have been enraptured with 'the light of the nineteenth century'—a wonderful luminary indeed, though slightly darkened by the follies, frauds and crimes which every day's newspaper reveals! [40]

But it is nothing new that the Church tries to borrow ideas and syncretize them into its beliefs, is it?

CHS No! We have had the light of scholarship, which praised Aristotle, and made the heathen author supply a textbook for Christian colleges.[41] We have heard more than enough of the light of the Church, in which we discern nothing except shades and conceits, borrowed from the medieval darkness of Christendom. But we have the trustworthy and the true when we hear, 'I am the light.' Where else shall light be found? Where shall bewildered men and women find a reliable guide? In the teaching of the person, the life, the death, the sacrifice of the Christ of Nazareth, we have the self-evident light, conspicuous by its own brilliance. Now he that follows Christ shall never walk in darkness. To follow him means to commit yourselves to him, to believe him, and yield yourselves up, obediently doing what he bids, and implicitly accepting what he says. Do not say, 'I will be taught by Calvin, Luther, Wesley, or anybody else.' Jesus Christ alone must be your light. His Word must be your sole authority.[42]

Please don't think this an aside, but some are content to accept that God brought everything into existence, like winding up a clockwork toy, and then let it go, but that he has no involvement in what the outcome is or will be.

CHS The notion of modern philosophers appears to be that the Lord has wound up the universe like a watch, and put it under his pillow, and gone to sleep. To me, such philosophy is dreary, for my soul aches for an infinite love which will give itself to me, and receive my love in return. I am orphaned if my Maker will not pity me as his child, and hear my prayers, wipe away my tears, and help and comfort me. Babies need a mother's heart as much as her hands. Can a child be properly brought up by machinery, washed by a millwheel, rocked by a pendulum, fed from a pipe, dressed by a steel hand, and committed to the care of a wonderful engine which could do everything except love? It would miss the eyes which weep, and smile, the lips which kiss and speak lovingly as it is embraced. No, I can neither accept a steam engine instead of my mother, nor a set of laws in exchange for my God.[43]

Thank you. Now let's move on to a further issue. From previous comments you seem sure that evolution is not here to stay?

CHS Within a few years the evolutionists will be cut in pieces by some new dreamers. The reigning philosophers of the present are so committed to their madness that they will be a perpetual subject of contempt. That which is now taught for a certainty will soon have been so disproved as to be trodden down as the mud in the streets. The Lord's truth lives and reigns, but man's inventions only last an hour.[44]

Are there any illustrations of this in history?

CHS Take the phrase, 'Your youth is renewed like the eagle's'

(Psalm 103:5). Socrates and the old naturalists used to say that when eagles grew old, they lost their old beak, talons and feathers, and became young again. People believed it in those times, but happily there is nobody who believes such rubbish now. I am quite sure David did not believe it! My persuasion is, the more I look into the Bible, though some have said it was only meant to teach religion, and that we must not expect accuracy in scientific facts, that they are mistaken. The Bible never makes a mistake in natural history, physics or anything else, but is as much inspired about one thing as about another.[45]

Perhaps you don't realize how powerful the evolutionary lobby is. Some of their spokespeople view creationists as dangerous in some way, and have said that we are not fit to be parents while we hold these views. Our position doesn't appear as hopeful as you are suggesting.

CHS If any of you live long enough you will see that the philosophy of today will be a football of contempt for the philosophy of that period. They will speak of evolution amidst roars of laughter; and the day will come, when children will look upon it as being the most foolish notion that ever crossed the human mind. So, you and I had better go on believing, and testing for ourselves, and proving the faithfulness of God, and living upon Christ our Lord, even though we see doubters come and go ad infinitum.[46]

Do you not think that the Bible can be read in any way at all that suggests evolution is the means by which God brought the living world into being?

CHS Not at all! I have already said, 'through faith we understand that the worlds were framed by the word of God, so that things which are seen were not made of things which do appear' (Hebrews 11:3). They have not evolved out of something that existed before. Evolution is a rank lie against revelation.[47]

So when the creation week was finished, what was the world like?

CHS In God's original empire everything was happiness, and joy, and peace …[48]

Then where did sin and death come from?

CHS Sin is a disease because it is not an essential part of man as he was created. It is something abnormal. It was not in human nature at first. 'God made man upright.' Our first parent, as he came fresh from the hand of his Maker, was without taint or speck of sin; he had a healthy body inhabited by a healthy soul. There was about him no tendency to evil; he was created pure and perfect. Sin does not enter into the constitution of man, per se, as God made it.[49]

So, you are saying then that death was not the means by which man ascended from ape creatures through an evolutionary process.

CHS Death is a part of Satan's dominion. He brought sin into the world when he tempted our mother Eve to eat the forbidden fruit, and with sin he also brought death into the world, with all its woes. If Satan had not tempted, perhaps man would have not revolted, and if he had not revolted he would have lived for ever. I think death is the devil's masterpiece. With the solitary exception of hell, death is certainly the most satanic mischief that sin hath accomplished. Nothing ever delighted the heart of the devil so much as when he found that the threat would be fulfilled, 'in the day that you eat of it you shall surely die'. And never was his malicious heart so full of hellish joy as when he saw Abel stretched upon the earth, slain by the club of his brother. 'Aha!' said Satan, 'this is the first of all intelligent creatures that has died. This is the crowning hour of my dominion. True, I have spoiled the glory of this earth, but this, this is my masterpiece; I have killed man; I have brought death into him, and here lies the first dead man.'[50]

So if death is unnatural for man, it is no wonder he fears it so much.

CHS It is very natural that man should fear to die, because he was not originally created to die. There was no reason why unfallen man should die, but now that we have sinned, the seeds of corruption are in our bodies, and it is appointed unto men once to die. Yet, as if the body knows that it is not according to the first decree of heaven that it should go to the earth and the worm, it has a natural reluctance to return to its last bed. This natural fear of death is not wrong.[51]

What a world of suffering we now live in, and it all traces back to that single act of sin in Eden. Thank God that the Saviour's sufferings are a complete remedy for sin.

CHS Yes, at the close of the six days' work of creation, God could say, of everything that he had made, that it was very good but, on the cross, the Saviour could not say, 'It is finished,' until his very heart had been broken with anguish and reproach. After man had fallen, God could not lift him up again without sighs, and groans, and bloody sweat—even death itself, the death of deaths, 'the death of the cross'.[52]

It seems to me that the great issue in all this is the question of what a person accepts as the authority in their life: the Bible, scientific theory or even their own ability to make judgements!

CHS You are right. With some their great source of belief is their own thought. They judge the divine revelation itself, and claim the right, not only to interpret it, but also to correct and expand it. In their complete self-confidence, they become judges of God's Word. They believe a doctrine because the present age confirms it or invents it. In their opinion, parts of Scripture are faulty, and need tinkering with scientific hammers.[53]

Do you have no sympathy for those who find believing in Christ difficult because of the arguments of evolution?

CHS I do not think there ever was a good reason for not believing in Christ. The most unreasonable things in all the world are doubt and unbelief. The modern scientist, who does not believe in the first chapter of the Book of Genesis, and who pours scorn upon the New Testament, believes things infinitely more incredible than he can ever detect in sacred Scripture. I do not hesitate to say that the whole theory of evolution is more monstrously false and foolish than any other ever conceived beneath high heaven, and it is a marvellous thing that men should be able to squeeze their minds into the belief of an absurdity which, in time to come, will be ridiculed to children in the schoolroom as an instance of the credulity of their ancestors.[54]

In closing this first interview, could we not, at least, make an alliance between creationists and theistic evolutionists for the sake of the gospel being preached? Can't we bury our differences for the sake of the bigger issue?

CHS My reply is another question. Does revelation teach us evolution? It never has struck me that the theory of evolution can, by any argument, be reconciled with the inspired record of the creation. You remember how it is distinctly stated, again and again, that the Lord made each creature 'after its kind' (Genesis 1:21, 24–25). Besides, I remind you that, after all these years in which so many people have been hunting up and down the world for 'the missing link' between animals and men, they have never discovered one monkey who has rubbed his tail off and ascended in the scale of creation so far as to take his place as the equal of the great family of mankind. Mr Darwin has never been able to find the germs of an Archbishop of Canterbury in the body of a goat, and I venture to prophesy that he will never accomplish such a feat. There are abundant evidences that one creature is like another in certain respects, for they are all the product of God's creative will; but what the advocates of evolution forget is that there is nowhere found a link showing development from one creature to another— there are breaks here and there, and so many missing links that the chain cannot be made complete. There are many resemblances between them, because they have all been wrought by the one great master-mind of God. Look at the similarities between the animal and the bird in the bat; think of the resemblance between a bird and a fish in the flying fish; yet, nobody, surely, would venture to tell you that a fish ever grew into a bird, or that a bat ever became a butterfly. Even where one species very closely resembles another, there is a speciality about each which distinguishes it from all others. I do not say that a person cannot believe in revelation and in evolution, too, for a man may believe what is infinitely wise and also what is completely stupid. In this evil age, there is apparently nothing that a man cannot believe he can believe.[55]

I take your answer to mean an unequivocal 'No!' We will take a break there.

Notes

1 Spurgeon thought evolution so ridiculous that he assumed its demise within 'another twenty years'. His hopes were not realized, but the scientific world has now split between gradualism and punctuated equilibrium. Neither theory has the slightest evidence supporting it. The latter was invented because there was no fossil evidence whatever for a gradual evolution. Perhaps Spurgeon's greatest fault here was to think the secular scientific fraternity honest enough to forsake a flawed theory.

2 From Spurgeon's autobiography: 'Opinions on subjects of general interest. Evolution. Reply to an enquiry about evolution theory.' 8 February 1887.

3 'Alone, Yet Not Alone', *MTP* 2271. John 16:31–32.

4 *Ibid.*

5 'The Perpetuity of the Gospel', *MTP* 2636. Luke 21:33.

6 *The Sword and the Trowel*, 1881. Life and Letters of Horace Bushnell. (This is a review by Spurgeon of *The life and letters of Horace Bushnell* in which this comment is contained as part of a witty criticism of Bushnell.)

7 *The Sword and the Trowel*, Volume 3, 1871.

8 A sermon given on 17 May 1857 at the Music Hall, Royal Surrey Gardens. 1 Corinthians 1:24.

9 'A Homily for Humble Folks', *MTP* 2140. Proverbs 30:2.

10 'The Modern Dead Sea, and the Living Waters', *MTP* 1852. Ezekiel 47:8.

11 *Ibid.*

12 'Light, Natural and Spiritual', *MTP* 660. Genesis 1:1–5.

13 'The First Day of Creation', *MTP* 1252. Genesis 1:4.

14 *Ibid.*

15 'Is Conversion Necessary?' *MTP* 1183. 2 Corinthians 5:17.

16 *Ibid.*

17 'The Problem of the Age', *MTP* 1885. Mark 8:4.

18 'An All-Rround Ministry': Addresses to Ministers and Students: What We Would Be?

19 'How to Become Fishers of Men', *MTP* 1906. Matthew 4:19.

20 'No Compromise', *MTP* 2047. Genesis 24:5–8.

21 'The Blood Shed for Many', *MTP* 1971. Matthew 26:28.

22 'Hideous Discovery', *MTP* 1911. Mark 7:20–23.

23 'The Very Bold Prophecy', *MTP* 1919. Isaiah 65:1.

24 'Servitude or Service—Which?' *MTP* 2306. 2 Chronicles 12:8.

25 C.H. Spurgeon, *Restoration of Truth and Revival*.

26 'Nathanael: or, the Man Needed for the Day', *MTP* 2068. John 1:47.

27 'Natural or Spiritual?' *MTP* 407. 1 Corinthians 2:14.

28 'Faith's Sure Foundation', *MTP* 1429. 1 Peter 2:6.

29 'Thy Rowers Have Brought Thee into Great Waters', *MTP* 1933. Ezekiel 27:26.

30 'Manasseh', *MTP* 105. 2 Chronicles 33:13.

31 'Sickness and Prayer, Healing and Praise', *MTP* 3274. Psalm 107:17–22.

32 Spurgeon originally said, 'in fifty years'.

33 'Idols Found Wanting, but Jehovah Found Faithful', *MTP* 2056. Isaiah 46:1–4.

34 This comment evidently comes from Spurgeon's awareness that Erasmus Darwin (grandfather of Charles Darwin), held that all things came from crustaceans. His coat of arms had a Latin inscription to this effect. It displays Spurgeon's knowledge of the history of the theory.

35 'Three Important Precepts', *MTP* 2152. Proverbs 23:19.

36 'Our Manifesto', *MTP* 2185. Galatians 1:11.

37 *The Sword and the Trowel.* June 1880. Inaugural Address at the 16th annual conference of The Pastors' College Association.

38 A type of insect, the larval stage of which lasts for two to three years, but as adults they live only for a day.

39 'The Light of the World', *MTP* 3534. John 8:12.

40 *Ibid.*

41 There are parallels between the history of science and its influence on the papal church and the acceptance of evolutionary theory since Darwin. Evolutionists ignore that it was Bible-believing men, like Kepler, who refused to accept the scientific theory of their day, that broke the hold of Aristotle's unscientific theories.

42 'The Light of the World', *MTP* 3534. John 8:12.

43 'The Commissariat of the Universe', *MTP* 3149. Psalm 104:28.

44 'My Own Personal Holdfast', *MTP* 2069. Micah 7:7.

45 'Our Youth Renewed', *MTP* 3417. Psalm 103:5.

46 'God Justified, though Man Believes Not', *MTP* 2255. Romans 3:3–4.

47 'Abraham, a Pattern to Believers', *MTP* 2292. Hebrews 11:9–10.

48 'The Destroyer Destroyed', *NPSP* 166. Hebrews 2:14.

49 'Christopathy', *MTP* 2499. Isaiah 53:5.

50 'The Destroyer Destroyed', *NPSP* 166. Hebrews 2:14

51 'Fear of Death', *MTP* 3125. Hebrews 2:15.

52 'New Tokens of Ancient Love', *MTP* 2880. Jeremiah 31:3.

53 'The Man Who Shall Never See Death', *MTP* 2169. John 8:51–53.

54 'Why Men Reject Christ', *MTP* 2463. Luke 9:52–53.

55 From Spurgeon's autobiography: 'Mr Spurgeon's Opinions on Subjects of General Interest. Evolution.' At one of the memorable gatherings under 'The Question Oak', a student asked Mr Spurgeon, 'Are we justified in receiving Mr Darwin's or any other theory of evolution?' The above is the answer.

On science and the Bible

In this interview I would like you to make some statements about the issue of science and the Bible. Please begin by summarizing your position on the Bible in the context of modern attempts to discredit it using science.

CHS The truth of God is the truth of God. What does it matter if scientists agree to our believing a part of the Bible? We believe it anyway. Their permission is no more important to our faith than the consent of the French to the English holding London. God being with us we will hold the whole of revealed truth, to the last.[1]

Again, to get a flavour of your position, please summarize how you view the theories and assumptions of science, and particularly Darwin's views.

CHS This century's philosophy will one day be spoken of as evidence that softening of the brain was very usual among its scientific men. We count the thought of the present moment to be methodical madness; and those who are furthest gone in it are gullible beyond imagination.[2]

What, then, should our response be when educated people undermine and discount the Bible all around us?

CHS The Bible is the book which has no errata in it. Neither in matters historical nor scientific does it blunder, any more than in matters theological. The mistake is with the man who thinks the Holy Spirit can be mistaken.[3]

Are you sure we may still have such confidence in its inerrancy and authority?

CHS Though the Bible has been twisted about by disrespectful hands, it is still the infallible revelation of God. It is a main part of our religion humbly to accept what God has revealed. Perhaps the highest form of adoration possible on this side of heaven is to bow our entire mental and spiritual being before the revealed mind of God. Let those who please worship science, reason, and their own judgements; it is ours to submit ourselves before the Lord our God.[4]

But has the Bible really come through the fire of criticism unscathed to allow us such unreserved submission?

CHS Some younger brethren have only tested the Scripture a little so far; but others of us, who are now getting grey, can assure them that we have tried the Word, as silver is tried in a furnace of earth; and it has stood every test. The sacred Word has endured more criticism than the best-accepted form of philosophy or science, and it has survived every ordeal. As one minister has said, 'After its present assailants are all dead, their funeral sermons will be preached from this Book—not one verse omitted—from the first page of Genesis to the last page of Revelation.' After using this sword of two edges upon coats of mail there is still no notch in its edge. It is neither broken nor blunted in the fight. Today it is still the selfsame mighty Word of God that it was in the hands of the Lord Jesus.[5]

I need to press you on this point. Are you certain that these new ideas have really left the Bible as trustworthy as ever?

CHS The Bible has passed through the furnace of persecution, literary criticism, philosophic doubt, and scientific discovery, and has lost nothing except those human interpretations clinging to it as alloy to precious ore.[6]

But it seems that science and the Bible conflict so often. What is the way forward for thinking men?

CHS To think is admirable, but not if we intend to use thought to supplement the teachings of Christ, or to improve on them, or to accommodate them to popular theories in science and philosophy. For my part, true science may say what it will, and never lack an attentive listener while I live. The more loudly it speaks the better, if it speaks facts and not theories, if it tells me what God has done and not what man has dreamed. All that true science can discover must tally with the word of revelation, because God speaks in nature precisely the same truth he has written in the Holy Scriptures. The evil is that 'wise men' add their own inferences to the facts as if they were of equal authority. What shall we do? Shall we alter the deductions of the fallible, or try to shape the declarations of the infallible? The question is not hard to answer. We are not to revise the statements of the Book, but the inferences of the philosophers. When philosophy contradicts revelation, what do I say? So much the worse for philosophy. It isn't the Word of God that is in error; the fault is on the other side.[7]

Could it not be that you are so prejudiced yourself that you are refusing to see the validity of certain scientific facts that discredit the Bible?

CHS I can truly say that my own experience and observation have confirmed the teachings of the Word of God. I have not yet met with anything which could shake my confidence in the divine revelation. I trust I am neither a complete fool nor a blind bigot, who would shut his eyes to reason. I would not ignore a certified fact in any department of knowledge, and yet I know of no fact which can disprove so much as one solemn declaration of God, nor even cast a shadow of suspicion upon a doctrine of Holy Scripture. I have heard much, but I have seen nothing of the science which disproves the Scriptures. There is no such science, it is an impostor which has stolen the name.[8]

You obviously believe unreservedly that we needn't adjust our message to accommodate the assertions of evolution.

CHS I abhor new gospels and new theologies. I am for that same ancient gospel which is said to be absolutely defunct today. They say science has wiped out the evangelicals—we are dead—we are gone. Happy are those who are not afraid to be on the side that is ridiculed and laughed at. Truth will have its turn, and though it now grinds the dust it shall be at the top before long, and those who are loyal to it will share its fortunes. Let us be bold enough to say, 'Put my name down among the fools who believe, and not among those whose wisdom lies in doubting everything.'9

Don't you ever feel a little vulnerable to rest your whole argument, faith and eternal destiny in the Bible only?

CHS I had rather have one little promise in the corner of the Bible to support my faith than I would have all the philosophies of scientific men to sustain my opinion. The history of philosophy is the history of fools. All the philosophers that have yet lived have been more successful in contradicting those that came before them than anything else.10

As we close this issue—that is, concerning the place of faith in the inerrancy of the Bible in relation to our belief in the literal view of Genesis 1—would it not be very reassuring if there was some unanswerable proof that it was all true?

CHS Has God said it? Then to ask any confirmation of it is a direct insult to him, a gratuitous impertinence against the majesty of heaven. Has God said it? Then we are bound to believe it more than if all the scientific men in the world for centuries had witnessed to it. Has God said it? Then we are more sure of it than if our reason proved it by mathematical demonstration. Has God said it? Then we are more certain of it than if we saw it with our eyes, for they might be deceived, or than if we heard it with our ears, for they might be mistaken.[11]

I stand rebuked! As we come to the end of our interview, what last word do you have for believers facing the issues of evolutionary thought as it seeks to erase creation from our Bibles and Christianity from our world?

CHS Keep going! With God the Holy Spirit helping you, resolve in your hearts this day that you will doubt all the boasted discoveries of science, all the affirmations of the wise, all the speculations of great thinkers, all your own feelings and all the conclusions drawn from outward circumstances, and everything that seems to be demonstrable to a certainty, but never, never, never, will you allow the thought to pass through your mind that God can ever run back from anything that he has spoken, or change the word that has gone forth from his lips.[12]

Notes

1 'The Greatest Fight in the World', Spurgeon's 'Final Manifesto'.

2 'The Cross Our Glory', *MTP* 1859. Galatians 6:14.

3 'These Three Things Go to the Making of a Proverb: Shortness, Sense and Salt', *Salt-cellars: Being a Collection of Proverbs. Together with Homely Notes Thereon*, Volume 2: M to Z.

4 Lecture given at the 16th annual conference of The Pastors' College Association, Tuesday 3 May 1881.

5 'The Greatest Fight In the World', Spurgeon's 'Final Manifesto'.

6 *The Treasury Of David,* Volume 1. Psalm 12:6.

7 'Forts Demolished and Prisoners Taken', *MTP* 1473. 2 Corinthians 10:5.

8 'As We Have Heard, So Have We Seen', *MTP* 2014.

9 'Recruits for King Jesus', *MTP* 1770. 1 Chronicles 12:16–18.

10 'My Own Personal Holdfast', *MTP* 2069. Micah 7:7.

11 'The True Position of the Witness Within', *MTP* 1428. 1 John 5:10.

12 'Mistrust of God Deplored and Denounced', *MTP* 1498. Numbers 14:11.

Attitudes to science

In this third interview I would like to explore your opinions and attitudes to the sciences in general. In our generation there is a growing creation science movement doing a great deal of excellent work providing support to those who have had their faith weakened or undermined by the all-pervading theory of evolution. Do you suppose that if such scientists could provide enough evidence to disprove evolution and to prove the Bible's trustworthiness, people would then not only give up their false views but also believe the gospel?

CHS Even if today a man should rise from his tomb, and come here to affirm the truth of the gospel, the unbelieving world would be no more near believing than it is now.[1]

What makes you say that so strongly?

CHS God's whole creation has already been ransacked by the hand of science, and has only testified to the truth of revelation. The whole history of buried cities and departed nations has preached out the truth that the Bible was true. Every strip of land in the far-off East has expounded and confirmed the prophecies of Scripture. If men are still unconvinced, do you suppose that one dead man rising from the tomb would convince them?[2]

How can the church survive this latest powerful attempt to destroy it if, as you say, no evidence is sufficient to refute it?

CHS The church has always been assailed with deadly errors. There is hardly a doctrine of our holy faith which has not been denied. Every age produces a new crop of heretics and doubters. Just as the current of the times may run, so the stream of unbelief changes its direction. We have lived long enough, some of us, to see three or four species of atheists and deists rise and die. They are short lived. We have seen the church attacked by weapons borrowed from geology, ethnology and anatomy. Fierce warriors have come from the schools of criticism, but she survives all her antagonists. In fact, the church has been enriched by the attacks, for her ministers have set to work to study the points that were undecided, to strengthen the walls that seemed weak, and so her towers have been strengthened, and her bulwarks consolidated. 3

If these attacks result in a stronger church, you must have every confidence that the church will do more than just survive.

CHS To disprove the Word of God and to overthrow Christianity is still the fond dream of wicked men, and therefore we expect even worse attacks. But as certainly as God has blown away these things like chaff before the wind in times gone by, so he will in the days to come.4

Let us turn to science and scientists then.

CHS As a general rule, science signifies bamboozlement, riding on hypotheses, or mystifying with long words.5

But there are many highly respected men who are fully persuaded of evolution.

CHS The most absurd theories will have their admirers if they come from men of great scientific attainments. [6]

But why do people not accept the facts? Why accept theories if they are so absurd or are contradicted by facts?

CHS Certain men's speculations are given credit because of their actual discoveries. But as real wealth often leads to ruinous speculations, so real scientific knowledge often leads to more than ordinary folly. Those to whom we should look for clear reasoning in natural science are the first to overleap its boundaries and to substitute their own daydreams for established facts. They may reason that they are descendants of apes, but have no right to say so of others. But they go further and say that as man came gradually from nothing, to nothing he gradually returns. 'If this doctrine,' says one book, 'as now held by a large and powerful section of the scientific world, does indeed, as it professes, afford the only plausible solution of the various problems of ontology, then it follows naturally and of necessity that matter is all-sufficient, and that man is an automaton without spirit or spontaneity. Then our immortality is a dream; volition, choice and responsibility are delusions; virtue, vice, right and wrong are sounds without possible meaning; and education, government, rewards and punishments are illogical and mischievous absurdities. Let us eat and drink, for tomorrow we shall be carbonic acid, water and ammonia.' We are thankful for the author's scientific refutation of such errors, and are yet more thankful that our own common sense upon these subjects still remains.[7]

Do you really believe that such intelligent and apparently rational scientists are blind to the obvious reality of the Creator and creation?

CHS If men despise the wisdom that is from above, how grievously God allows them to prove their own ignorance! When men will not receive Scripture's testimony concerning God's creation, they immediately begin to form theories that are a thousand times more ridiculous, for God leaves them, if they will not accept his solution of the problem, to grope for another, and their own solution is so absurd, that all the world except themselves has sense enough to laugh at it.[8]

But when evolutionists hear Christians say such things they say that we belong with those who opposed Galileo—despite the fact that it was his scientific peers who opposed him and Bible believers who supported his methodology.[9]

CHS 'They say, they say,' and donkeys bray. Common talk is really no more to be regarded than the braying of asses. The theoretical talk of unbelieving scientists may be put in the same category. Think of this as taught by science:

> Man was an ape in the days that came early;
> Centuries after his hair became curly:
> Centuries more gave a thumb to his wrist,
> Then he became man and a Positivist.[10]

What is your advice to such scientists? After all, they seem pretty sure that evolution, in one form or other, is how we arrived here.

CHS Beware of spurious wisdom, for there is much abroad in the world of 'science falsely so called'. Hypotheses are invented, and facts are manufactured, or at least coloured, to sustain them, and then for a while the academic world goes mad upon its new theory, and we are solemnly warned that we must not be opposed to the spirit of the age. However, in a short time, a fresh hypothesis shoves the former one from its perch, and the wisdom of yesterday is shown to be foolishness and goes into the limbo of the ten thousand equally absurd infallibilities which have preceded it.[11]

Do you think that educated men really can be so gullible as to either be taken in by such a fraud as evolution, or to choose to believe a lie?

CHS Some men will believe any monstrous assertion of scientists, or spiritualists, or rationalists; but they cannot believe the plain witness of the Lord Jesus Christ.[12]

Sometimes they say they have reached definite and provable conclusions that are clearly in conflict with the Bible. Should we not accept what is proved?

CHS No one is more ready than I am to accept the evident facts of science. But what do you mean by science? Is 'science' infallible? Is it not science 'falsely so-called'? The history of that human ignorance which calls itself 'philosophy' is absolutely identical with the history of fools, except where it diverges into madness. If another Erasmus were to arise and write the history of folly, he would have to give several chapters to philosophy and science, and those chapters would be more telling than any others.[13]

But does modern science really contradict itself, more than it contradicts the Word of God as you suggest?

CHS Let the wise of each generation speak of the previous generation, for there are few theories in science today which will survive. We travel at so rapid a rate that we rush by sets of scientific hypotheses as quickly as we pass telegraph posts when riding in an express train. All we can be sure of today is that what the learned were sure of a few years ago is now thrown into the limbo of discarded errors. I have said before that no proven fact in nature is opposed to revelation. The fanciful part of science, so dear to many, is what we do not accept.[14]

But surely scientists are more interested in fact than what you call fancy: the theories and speculations?

CHS On the contrary, that is the important part of science to many—that part which is a mere guess, for which the guessers fight tooth and nail. The mythology of science is as false as the mythology of the heathen, but they make this their god.[15]

What harm can come, though, from believers delving into evolution and trying to see where it leads?

CHS Two kinds of people have wrought great mischief, and neither are worth considering judges in the matter: they are both disqualified. The first is the irreligious scientist. What does he know about religion? What can he know? He is out of court when the question is 'Does science agree with religion?' Obviously he who wishes to answer this query must know both the things in question. The second is a better man, but capable of still more mischief. I mean the unscientific Christian who tries to reconcile the Bible with science. He had better leave it alone, and not begin tinkering. The mistake made by such men has been that in trying to solve a difficulty, they have either twisted the Bible, or contorted science. Then we hear the cry that Scripture has been defeated. Not at all! It is only a wrong interpretation which has been removed.[16]

Give me an example of what you mean.

CHS Someone might write a book to prove that the six days of creation represent six geological periods. He shows how the geological strata, and the organisms in them, follow very much in the order of the Genesis story of creation. It may be so, or it may not be so; but if anybody should before long show that the strata do not lie in any such order, what would be my reply?[17]

I don't know.

CHS I should say that the Bible never taught that they did. There is nothing said about long ages of time. On the contrary, 'the evening and the morning were the first day', and 'the evening and the morning were the second day'; and so on. If such a book is all fudge, the Bible is not responsible for it. It is true that his theory has an appearance of support from the parallelism which he makes out between the organic life of the ages and that of the seven days; but this may be accounted for from the fact that God usually follows a certain order whether he works in long periods or short ones. I do not know, and I do not care, much about the question; but I want to say that, if you demolish such an explanation you must not imagine that you have damaged the scriptural truth which seemed to require the explanation: you have only burned the wooden palisades with which well-meaning men thought to protect an impregnable fort which needed no such defence. For the most part, we had better leave a difficulty where it is, rather than make another difficulty by our theory. Why make a second hole in the kettle, to mend the first? Especially when the first hole is not there at all. Believe everything in science which is proved: it will not come to much. You need not fear that your faith will be overburdened. And then believe everything which is clearly in the Word of God, whether it is proved by outside evidence or not. No proof is needed when God speaks. If he has said it, this is evidence enough.[18]

What do you say to those who may think you oppose all research and scientific investigation?

CHS We are ready to accept all that science teaches us when it has made up its mind what it is. We never despise knowledge, but we do not want to be duped by conjectures and fooled by speculations. We are glad to receive all that intelligent minds can discover for us concerning the wonderful works of the Lord, but we must beware of spurious imitations. [19]

I ask again, is it really possible for educated men to be so completely mistaken?

CHS There are learned men—and learned men. One class of know-alls mistake assertion for proof, and sneering for logic; from such we turn away. It is written of certain people, 'professing themselves to be wise, they became fools' (Romans 1:22), and we know the family is not extinct; therefore we look before we leap.[20]

But, do not these highly qualified men and women despise the lack of knowledge of most believers in Christ? They seem to believe it is because we are ignorant, or less well educated that we hold to the old teaching of creation.

CHS We are not such wonderful know-alls as certain of our neighbours. They may push off into the sea of speculation; our smaller boats must hug the shore of certainty. To us, however, it is no small comfort that the Lord has revealed to babes the things which are hidden from the wise and prudent.[21]

Isn't there another side to this though? If there is the danger of being led away from Christ through the study of science, is it not better to avoid it altogether, especially as it seems they lead in opposing directions?

CHS Let not science and religion be reckoned as opposing citadels, frowning defiance at each other. They have too many common foes, such as ignorance and prejudice, passion and vice, under all their forms, to permit wasting their strength in a useless warfare with each other. Science has a foundation, and so has religion; let them unite their foundations, and the basis will be broader, and they will be two compartments of one great framework reared to the glory of God. In the one, let all look, and admire and adore; and in the other, let those who have faith kneel, and pray, and praise. Let the one be the sanctuary where human learning may present its richest incense as an offering to God, and the other the holiest of all, separated from it by a veil now rent in two, and in which, on a blood sprinkled mercy-seat, we pour out the love of a reconciled heart, and hear the oracles of the living God.[22]

So you don't think believers are better avoiding the study of the sciences?

CHS Not at all! I wish we were all instructed after the order of true science, which deals with nature itself, and not with theories.[23]

I understand there have been many men of history whose study of science led them to an even deeper reverence for God.

CHS The mighty Newton, a true prince among men, was continually driven to his knees as he looked upwards to the skies, and discovered fresh wonders in the starry heavens. The science which tends to bring men to bow in humility before the Lord should always be a favourite study with those whose business it is to inculcate reverence for God in all who come under their influence.[24]

Is it possible then for science to lead us to a perfect knowledge of God?

CHS The god whom men find out for themselves is not the true God. I think that this day it is true, as in Paul's day, 'The world by wisdom did not know God' (1 Corinthians 1:21). You may as well search for the springs of the sea, as expect to find out God by science. I often hear people say, 'They go from nature up to nature's God.' It is a very long step—too far for human strength. It is far easier to go from nature's God to nature, and far safer to believe in him who stoops out of the heavens, and reveals himself to you.[25]

But some say that the magi were the scientists of their day, and they found a way to Christ! What do you think of that idea?

CHS Their philosophy was not a very true one; it was about as true as modern philosophy, which is not saying much. They believed very absurd things, these magi, almost as absurd as the scientists of the present day, perhaps not quite as ridiculous, for science has grown in absurdity, especially of late.[26]

So why should a Christian devote himself to such a study?

CHS If he cultivates science, it is to be that he may the more successfully explain and vindicate the gospel.[27]

I know a number of scientists who seek to strengthen the churches by doing this very thing.

CHS A scientific man does great service when he sanctifies his science by pointing out the traces of the divine handiwork. While others see only the creation, he goes further, and sees the Creator.[28]

Is there a value, then, in lectures on science from the Christian viewpoint?

CHS I never decry popular lectures on scientific or historical subjects. If the lectures maintain a Christian tone, much good will come of them.[29]

Do you think the world will really sit up and pay attention when Christians who are also eminent scientists are heard on the media or in creation apologetic meetings?

CHS If a scientific man is of unbelieving principles he is cried up as an eminent thinker and discoverer; but should he be a true Christian, and know twenty times as much as his fellows, he is called a person of antiquated views and narrow notions.[30]

One of these opponents of creation said words to the effect, 'I had motives for not wanting the world to have a meaning; consequently assumed that it had none, and was able without any difficulty to find satisfying reasons for this assumption.'[31] Such statements reveal not merely previously held mental presuppositions, but moral prejudice.

CHS Nothing stands so much in the way of real knowledge as prejudice. Our race might have known a great deal more of scientific fact if it had not been so largely occupied and captivated with scientific supposition. Take up books upon most sciences, and you will find that the main part of the material is an answer to divers theories that have been set up in ages gone by, or originated in modern times. Theories are the nuisances of science; the rubbish which must be swept away that the precious facts may be laid bare. If you go to study a subject saying to yourself, 'This is how the matter must shape itself,' having beforehand made up your mind what the facts ought to be, you will have put in your way a more severe difficulty than even the subject could place there. Prejudice is the stumbling block of advance. To believe that we know before we do know is to prevent our really making discoveries and coming to right knowledge.[32]

Have you any word of caution to scientists who are so confident that they have arrived at the ultimate foundation for truth, when they speak so confidently of Darwin's theory?

CHS I say again, see how often science has altered its very basis! Science is notorious for being most scientific in destruction of all the science that has gone before it. I have sometimes indulged myself, in leisure moments, in reading ancient natural history, and nothing can be more humorous.[33]

In closing, what have you to say to those who devote themselves to the sciences and yet do not believe in a Creator?

CHS In looking on the works of God in creation, there are two questions which at once occur to the thoughtful mind, and which must be answered before we can gain a clue to the philosophy and science of creation itself. The first one is the question of authorship: Who made all these things? And the next question is that of design: For what purpose were all these things created?[34]

Is the argument of design so significant?

CHS Is it not one of the clearest arguments for Godhead that design is visible everywhere? Take the smallest animal or most minute insect, and you will find in it the most admirable contrivances to suit the habits of the creature and to make it happy in its condition. These creatures not only show design, but supply proof that the design works excellently. No creature has to go to its Creator and complain, 'There is a defect in my structure; I cannot carry out the purpose for which I was designed.' Our own bodies, too, have about them, if we will observe them, ten thousand proofs of the surpassing foresight and masterly art of the great Maker. Oh that being so wonderfully made by God we might feel bound to show forth his praise![35]

Yes! Design requires a designer. It is not only a powerful argument for the being of God, but it shows why man is always trying to find or give meaning to life, doesn't it?

CHS Yes! All creation is full of traces of design.[36]

So do you believe that if we can present the reasons well enough we shall win the argument about origins?

CHS The facts about creation must be the subject of faith. It is true that they can be substantiated, by the argument from design, and in other ways; still, for a wise purpose as I believe, God has not made even that matter of the creation of the universe perfectly clear to human reason, so there is room for the exercise of faith. Men like to have everything laid down according to the rules of mathematical precision, but God desires them to exercise faith; and, therefore, he has not acted according to their wishes.[37]

Thank you. Our fourth interview will attempt to help our young people as they face this issue in schools and universities.

Notes

1 'A Preacher from the Dead', *NPSP* 143. Luke 16:31.

2 *Ibid.*

3 'The Arrows of the Bow Broken in Zion', *MTP* 791. Psalm 76:3.

4 *Ibid.*

5 'The Spirit and the Wind', *MTP* 2067. John 3:8.

6 *The Sword and The Trowel*, 1877. Book review of Charles Elam and M.D. Smith, *Winds of Doctrine.*

7 *Ibid.*

8 'Search The Scriptures', *NPSP* 172. Isaiah 8:20.

9 Johannes Kepler, a Bible-believing Christian, not only was a friend of Galileo, but was the probable deliverer who saved him from the criticism of his day. In reality, the false theories of science held by scientists and accepted by the church of the day *jointly* opposed Galileo. It is simply rewriting history to say it was only the (Roman Catholic) Church that was hostile to the scientist. It was the unwillingness of other scientists to face the evidence Galileo produced that created the problem. The church had merely absorbed the scientific errors of its day. (History does repeat itself!) The evidence of Galileo contradicted those long-held theories. His method of experimentation and observation was, in fact, unique among his scientific peers who blindly followed the errors of Aristotle and others. Bible-believers of that generation discovered the laws proving beyond doubt that Aristotle and others were in error. The apostate church had made a false step in adopting false views and was justly discredited when the scientists moved on to other theories. Theologians of today do well to learn from history. It is also a further example in history of eisegesis (interpreting the Bible by an authority outside the text) rather than exegesis, (interpreting Scripture by Scripture).

10 'These Three Things Go to the Making of a Proverb: Shortness, Sense and Salt', *op. cit.*

11 'The Bible and The Newspaper', *Spurious Imitations.*

12 'Christ's Testimony Received', *MTP* 2158. John 3:33.

13 'The Greatest Fight in the World', Spurgeon's 'Final Manifesto'.

14 *Ibid.*

15 *Ibid.*

16 *Ibid.*

17 *Ibid.*

18 *Ibid.*

19 'The Bible and the Newspaper', *Spurious Imitations.*

20 *Ibid.*

21 'Preparation for the Coming of the Lord', *MTP* 2105. 1 John 2:28.

22 *The Treasury of David.* Psalm 19.

23 'The Sweet and the Sweetener', *MTP* 2403. Psalm 104:34.

24 'The Sciences as Sources of Illustration. Astronomy: The Pastors' College, President's Lecture 7', *Lectures to My Students.*

25 'The Keynote of the Year', *MTP* 2121. Psalm 103:1.

26 'The Far-off, Near; the Near, Far Off', *MTP* 2325. Matthew 2:1–4.

27 'Christ Crucified', *MTP* 2673. 1 Corinthians 2:2.

28 'Declaring the Works of the Lord', *MTP* 2540. Psalm 118.17.

29 'Penny Readings or a Snake in the Grass', *The Sword and The Trowel*, October 1867.

30 'A Sermon upon One Nothing by Another Nothing', *MTP* 1458. 2 Corinthians 12:11.

31 Aldous Huxley, *Confessions of a Professed Atheist,* Report: Perspective on the News, Volume 3, June 1966, p.19.

32 'The New Fashion', *MTP* 1269. Mark 2:12.

33 'Our Manifesto', *MTP* 2185. Galatians 1:11.

34 'Why Are Men Saved?' *NPSP* 115. Psalm 106:8.

35 'A Feast for Faith', *MTP* 711. Isaiah 28:29.

36 *Ibid.*

37 'Unbelievers Upbraided', *MTP* 2890. Mark 16:14.

Advice to young people

Have you anything to encourage both the young person at school being taught evolution as fact, and the anxious parent or pastor who sees its influence so deeply embedded in our culture?

CHS Now, in the lives of even some of the younger folks here you might have seen in England different systems of unbelief coming up in different quarters, under which the thinkers of the age (as they call themselves), or the triflers of the hour (as we might better style them), have sought shelter. At one time we were all wrong because of some wonderful discovery of old bones. Geology had upset us. Then some other science was brought to the front. I have lived to see a number of little scares. As to the present pretensions, whatever they may be, we have only to wait a little while with confidence in God, and we shall see them also wither away. Yes, and if there were to be systems of unbelief in the world more enduring, colossal as the Alps, with foundations deep as hell, we still need only to exercise faith enough and cry to God loudly enough, and fling ourselves upon Omnipotence boldly enough, and then to speak, and in the speaking of the everlasting gospel we shall see these mountainous systems plucked up by the roots and cast into the midst of the sea. There is the point: we must have divine strength to do it.[1]

So, do young people come and discuss this issue with you then?

CHS Certain young folks say to me, 'I have read a new book: there is a great discovery made about evolution. Animals were not created separately, but grew out of one another by degrees of gradual improvement.' Go and ask your grandmother about it! And what does she say as she takes off her spectacles? Why, she says, 'I was reading, "There shall come in the last days scoffers, walking after their own lusts."' (2 Peter 3:3). Say to her, 'Do you not feel alarmed about your faith?' 'No,' she says, 'if they were to discover fifty thousand things, it would not trouble me, for "I know whom I have believed, and am persuaded that he is able to keep that which I have committed unto him against that day"' (2 Timothy 1:12). You think her a simpleton, perhaps: she might far more properly think you the same.[2]

But these same young people may be laughed at in school. What if they are called old-fashioned and thought to be complete fools for holding to outdated beliefs?

CHS Be content to be old-fashioned. Some will despise you for your simplicity, and insinuate that you are destitute of culture and science, and are repeating exploded dogmas only believed in by the illiterate. This refutes itself, for the truly wise never show contempt of others. Hold to God's truth, whoever challenges it.[3]

Let's think about young people who have the capacity for study, especially in the sciences. What more can you say to encourage them?

CHS Labour to know God in his actions. Study the past. Do not be ignorant of the great work of creation. If you have the skill, look at creation in the light of modern science so far as that light is really derived from fact and not conjecture. Pry into God's great works in providence. Begin your pilgrimage of study at the gates of Eden and travel onward to the present time; float safely in your meditations with Noah in the ark; study the wonderful justice of God in thus sweeping away the race of men.4

Such study cannot lead us to understand and appreciate everything about the universe. After all, the Bible speaks about angels, devils, heaven and hell. These cannot be investigated by science, can they?

CHS That is one of the earliest lessons of faith. We do not discover the secrets of creation by mere reason, or the teachings of science; it is only by revelation that the marvellous story can reach us. Faith accepts the inspired declaration that God made all things, so that, after all, the foundation of everything is that which is not seen.5

It is very discouraging for those setting out in following Christ to have so much hostility against the very foundation of their whole faith. How can we help those who are tempted to doubt because of the strength of the opinions of the evolutionists?

CHS There are dreamers nowadays who cast doubt on everything. Taking to themselves the name of philosophers, and professing to know something of science, they make statements worthy only of idiots, and demand for their self-evidently false assertions the assent of rational men. The word 'philosopher' will soon come to mean a lover of ignorance, and the term 'a scientific man' will be understood as meaning a fool, who has said in his heart there is no God. Such attacks upon the eternal verities of our holy faith can have no effect upon hearts so taken up with love for the Son of God, for, dwelling in his immediate presence, they have passed the stage of doubt, left the region of questioning far behind, and in this matter have entered into rest.[6]

Don't you wish they didn't have to face such thorny issues as evolution?

CHS There are pearls in oyster shells, and fruits on thorny boughs. The paths of true science, especially natural history and botany, abound with blessing. Geology, so far as it is fact, and not fiction, is full of treasures. History is eminently instructive. Follow the trails of knowledge, according as you have the time, the opportunity, and the ability. And do not hesitate to do so because you fear educating yourselves up to too high a point. When grace abounds, learning will not puff you up, or injure your simplicity in the gospel. Serve God with such education as you have, and thank him for blowing through you if you are a ram's horn, but if there be a possibility of your becoming a silver trumpet, go for it! [7]

How can they avoid falling into error?

CHS We must learn to discriminate, and that point needs insisting on. Many run after novelties. Learn to judge between truth and its counterfeits and you will not be led astray. Others adhere like limpets to old teachings, and yet these may only be ancient errors:

prove all things, and hold fast to what is good. The use of the sieve, and the winnowing fan, is much to be commended.[8]

But some young people do end up with doubts and questions. What should they do about these problems?

CHS If at any time you find the truth of God is assailed, and your own mind is filled with doubt about some doctrine, always ask God to open that particular truth to your understanding. Trials often burn doctrines into us in such a way that they become as precious to us as a gift which we could never part with. Opposition to the truth often leads to the increase of evidence in its support. The outcome will be that the more we are assaulted with the arguments of science, falsely so-called, the firmer we will adhere to the oracles of God.[9]

So, they are to pray for God's help in understanding the truth of the Bible. Is there anything else that may help them?

CHS Walk humbly with God in studying his Word and in believing his truth. There are a number of men, nowadays, who are critics of the Bible. It is brought as a criminal to their court. It lies on their table to be dissected, and they will cut out its very heart. The precious Song of Solomon, John's Gospel or the Book of Revelation, is not sacred in their eyes. They shrink from nothing. Their scalpel cuts through everything. They are the judges of what the Bible ought to be, and it is deposed from its throne. Don't be like that but ever desire to sit at the feet of God in the Scriptures. [10]

A teachable, not a gullible spirit is a precious attribute, but it does rely on the Bible being completely without error, doesn't it?

CHS I do not believe that, from one cover to the other, there is any mistake in it of any sort whatever, either upon natural or physical science, or upon history or anything whatever. [11]

I can hear some people saying that it isn't necessary to believe in an inerrant Bible to be a Christian. What do you say to them?

CHS I am prepared to believe whatever it says, and to take it believing it to be the Word of God; for if it is not all true, it is not worth a single penny to me. It may be worth something to someone who is clever enough to pick out the true from the false, but I am such a fool that I could not do that. If I do not have a guide here that is infallible, I would as soon guide myself, for I shall have to do so anyway. If I have to continually correct the blunders of my guide, which I am not qualified to do, I am worse off than if I had no guide at all. [12]

Let's get down to the real issue though. We are told that science contradicts or has disproved the Bible. The Bible says God created everything from nothing, and science says that matter is eternal, that there was a Big Bang, and that man came from monkeys. What is the answer to these assertions of the atheists?

CHS My first point is that between the revelation of God in his Word, and that in his works, there can be no actual discrepancy. One may go further than the other, but they must be harmonious.

Between the *interpretation* of the works and the *interpretation* of the Word there may be very great differences. We must frankly admit that the men of the Book have sometimes missed its meaning: we have never held the doctrine of the infallibility of Scripturists. It is also obvious that, in their desire to defend their Bible, devout persons have been unwise enough to twist its words, or, at least, to give them an unnatural meaning, in order to make it agree with the teachings of scientific men. This has been their weakness. If they had always laboured to understand what God said in his Book, and had steadfastly stuck to its meaning, whatever might be advanced by scientists, they would have been wiser. As professed science advances towards real science the fact that the old Book is right would also have become increasingly apparent to them.

Secondly, remember that scientific facts are not infallible Those who have addicted themselves to the study of nature, and have despised the Word, cannot claim such immunity from error as to demand the interpretation of Scripture to be revised every time they enthrone a new hypothesis. The history of philosophy reads very like a Comedy of Errors, each generation refuting its predecessors. There is therefore every probability that much of what is now endorsed as orthodox scientific doctrine will be entirely upset in a few years' time.

Thirdly, remember that there is very little that is settled in science. There are many voices in the world, some powerful, and others weak; but there is not a sufficiently strong consensus to demonstrate any one system of science to be absolutely true. These good people have done their best, from Aristotle downwards, but they have hardly accomplished more than to prove us all dunces, and themselves scarcely a fig better than the rest of us.

Fourthly, instead of altering the Bible, or allowing that it may be mistaken in mundane matters, it is far safer to continue the ongoing process of amending science, which is made of a substance so pliable that no great effort is required to change its form to the reverse of its present shape. From the first doctor in the school of science down to the last, the limitation of human faculties and the mystery of phenomena, means error has not only been possible, but almost unavoidable. Even the interpreters of Scripture have been less absurd than the interpreters of Nature. The Book still retains its impregnable position. If it ever comes to a choice between whether I believe God's revelation or man's science, I shall unhesitatingly cry, 'Let God be true, and every man a liar' (Romans 3:4).

Fifthly, be aware that there really is no great difficulty. Scripture may not square with certain hypotheses, but it agrees with facts. The Scripture, interpreted in an intelligent manner, displays as complete an agreement with Nature and Providence as Words can show with Works.

Lastly, remember that when the Bible is fully accepted as God's own revelation of himself, the mind has come to a quiet anchorage; and this is no small gain. A safe resting-place is the urgent need of the soul. To find a firm roothold somewhere, men have tried to rest in an infallible church, or in their own supposed infallible reason. I prefer to cast anchor once and for all in an infallible revelation.[13]

I am sure that advice is sound. But remember, not everyone has the same knowledge of the Bible as you do. Young people, especially, may find themselves unsettled by new discoveries or new theories in science.

CHS I remember with what alarm some of my friends received the tidings of the geological discoveries of modern times, which did not quite agree with their interpretation of Moses' history of creation. They thought it an awful thing that science should discover something which seemed to contradict the Scriptures. Well, we lived over the geological difficulty, after all. Since then there have been different sets of philosophic infidels, who have risen up and made wonderful discoveries, and poor timid Christians thought, 'What a terrible thing! This will be the end of true Christianity. When science brings facts against us, how shall we stand?' They only had to wait about another week, and suddenly they found that science was not their enemy but their friend, for the truth, though tried in a furnace like silver, is ever the gainer by the trial.[14]

I remember thinking certain statements were even contradictory, until I understood them more fully. I found that I had to trust where I did not fully understand. Was that the correct way forward?

CHS Sometimes you will meet with a teaching of God's Word which you do not understand. You cannot reconcile it with some other truth, or see, perhaps, how it glorifies God. Then we glorify God by believing it.[15]

But what if a teaching from the Bible seems unreasonable?

CHS To believe a doctrine which you see to be true by mere reason is nothing very wonderful. There is no very great glory to God in believing what is as clear as the sun in the heavens, but to believe a truth when it staggers you—that is the sort of believing we ought to exercise towards God. I do not see the fact, and I cannot quite apprehend it, but God says it is so, and I believe him.[16]

But, it may be that teachers or lecturers, even at so-called Church schools, will tell us that we are extremists and have set ourselves against all the thinkers, philosophers and scientists of our age.

CHS If all the philosophers in the world should contradict the Scriptures, so much the worse for them. Their contradiction makes no difference to my faith. Half a grain of God's word weighs more than a thousand tons of words or thoughts of all the modern theologians, philosophers, and scientists that exist on the face of the earth, for God knows more about his own works than they do. They only *think*, but the Lord *knows*.[17]

What about when a scientist's educational qualifications are used to intimidate us in an attempt to make us change our views of the story of Creation?

CHS They are no more qualified to judge than the poorest man in the church of God. Inasmuch as the most educated unregenerate men are dead in sin, what do they know about the things of God? Instead of setting them to judge I would sooner trust our boys and girls that have just been converted, for they do know something of divine things.[18]

I remember one person derisively asking me what Boy Scouts' certificate I had, compared with the learning and eminence of a theologian who denied the creation account as history and also the eternal punishment of the lost.

CHS This style of argument I have heard even in these days. We are expected to give up the faith because scientists condemn it, and they are such eminent persons that we ought to accept their dictates without further delay. I confess I am not prepared to accept their infallibility any more than that which hails from Rome.[19]

So, as we move to the end of this interview, you said earlier that young people should focus on their walk with God, their quiet times and additional times of Bible reading and prayer as they face the opposition of teachers and friends who deride them for not accepting evolution.

CHS God's name, dear friends, is revealed in a measure in nature and in providence, but David tells us that the Lord has magnified his Word above all his name. That is to say, special revelation[20] is made by God to be infinitely superior to creation and to providence as a revealing of himself.[21]

How is Scripture so superior in revealing God to us?

CHS If a man paints grand pictures, even if I never saw the man, I know a little about him when I see his paintings, but if he writes me a letter, and in that letter tells me what is in his very heart, I know more about him by his words than I do by his works. There is more of God in some passages of the Bible than in the whole universe together. If science could be all known, it would not contain as much real light as there is in a single verse of Scripture, for the best light is in the Word. Other lights are only moonlight compared with the sunlight. God has magnified his Word, for its clearness, above every other method of revealing his name or character.[22]

Some of our young people have thought that science is the reality and faith in the Bible is make-believe.

CHS Rest assured that this is not constructing castles in the air, for our faith is no delusion, but is made of solid, substantial stuff, before which even the supposed infallibilities of science are as light as air.[23]

The Bible states that the evidence of creation leaves atheists without excuse, however they claim that theirs is a rational position. Do they really know there is a God?

CHS It is marvellous what effect the thunder has had upon all kinds of men. The most wicked of men have been forced to acknowledge that there must be a Creator, when they have heard that marvellous voice of his sounding through the sky. Men of the stoutest nerve and the boldest blasphemy have become the weakest of all creatures, when God has made himself known in the mighty whirlwind, or storm.[24]

So, our young people have to face these battles. It is obvious that God permits these as a test of our faith.

CHS Yes, the test will come again and again. May the gibes of adversaries only make us ready for the sterner ordeals of the judgement to come. Examine your Christianity. You have a great quantity, some of you, but what of its quality? Can your religion stand the test of poverty, scandal and scorn? Can it stand the test of scientific sarcasm and contempt? Will your religion stand the test of long sickness of body and depression of spirit caused by weakness?[25]

How serious is it when people try to dissuade young people from taking the Bible at face value and believing it from cover to cover?

CHS What an accumulation of guilt must be resting upon the mind of the man who breathes out doubt as other men breathe air! See how he blasts the souls on whom he breathes! Calculate his crimes. Put down the soul-murders of which he is guilty. For example, a young man decoyed from the Bible-class, familiarized with blasphemous ideas, and then led into outward sin and speedy death. Write that down in blood. Note the next example. A young girl, once hopeful but then impressed by the supposed scientific knowledge of an unbeliever, led from the faith of her mother, and by-and-by snared by the world so as to live and die impenitent. Write that also in blood to be demanded at the doubter's door in the last great day! May God give repentance to those who have been doing the Devil's murderous work with both their hands by denying the truth and sowing the seeds of unbelief! If I speak to any such, I do it with sorrowful indignation, and I beg them to turn from their evil way.[26]

Thank you. That is a very serious note on which to end this interview.

Notes

1 'The Moral of a Miracle', *MTP* 1444. Mark 11:22.

2 'Knowledge Commended', *MTP* 609. Daniel 11:32–33.

3 'David Dancing before the Ark because of His Election', *MTP* 2031. 2 Samuel 6:20–22.

4 'Knowledge Commended', *MTP* 609. Daniel 11:32–33.

5 'Jesus Only—a Communion Meditation', *MTP* 2634. Mark 9:8.

6 'A Song among the Lilies', *MTP* 1190. Song of Solomon 2:16.

7 'Necessity of Minsterial Progress: Lecture 2', *Lectures to My Students.*

8 *Ibid.*

9 'Prosperity under Persecution', *MTP* 997. Exodus 1:10–12.

10 'Micah's Message for Today', *MTP* 2328. Micah 6:8.

11 *Ibid.*

12 *Ibid.*

13 Selections from *The Clue of the Maze: Science and the Book at One.*

14 'The Security of the Church', *NPSP* 161. Psalm 125:2.

15 'The Key-note of a Choice Sonnet', *MTP* 1514. Luke 1:46.

16 *Ibid.*

17 *Ibid.*

18 *Ibid.*

19 'Our Lord's First Appearance before Pilate', *MTP* 1644. John 18:38.

20 Special Revelation is that resulting in, and now solely contained within the sixty-six books of the Old and New Testaments.

21 'Open Praise and Public Confession', *MTP* 2604. Psalm 138:1–3.

22 *Ibid.*

23 'Thought-reading Extraordinary', *MTP* 1802. Psalm 10:17.

24 'His Majestic Voice', *NPSP* 87. Psalm 29:4.

25 'Let Him Deliver Him Now', *MTP* 2029. Matthew 27:43.

26 'Jesus and the Children', *MTP* 1925. Mark 10:13–16.

Comments for preachers

In this interview I want to explore advice for gospel ministers in our own day. There is pressure on preachers, especially in university towns or connected with reaching out to students, to retain their intellectual credibility by siding in some areas with their opponents, especially in relation to controversies like the creation-evolution debate.

CHS Much as I love true science and real education, I mourn and grieve that ministers dilute the Word of God with philosophy, desiring to be intellectual preachers, delivering model sermons, fitted for a room full of college students and professors of theology, but of no use to the masses, because they are destitute of simplicity, warmth, earnestness, or even solid gospel matter.[1]

Do you not think it adds weight to our argument when we can show that highly qualified scientists or well-educated ministers can argue the case for creation?

CHS To be reputed wise is the heaven of most mortals. To win a degree, and wear half-a-dozen letters of the alphabet at the end of your name, is the glory of many. To me the fashion seems cumbersome, but the grand use of these appended letters is to let the world know that this is a man who knows more than others. However, it is more magnanimous to do without the certificates, and let folks find out for themselves that you possess unusual information. One should not know merely to have it known that you know.[2]

I suppose it is easy to be distracted from the main issue of the gospel.

CHS It must have been hard for the apostle to determine to keep to his one subject, 'Jesus Christ, and him crucified'. Nine-tenths of the ministers of this age could not have done it. Fancy Paul going through the streets of Corinth, and hearing a philosopher explain the current theory of creation. He is telling the people something about the world springing out of certain things that previously existed, and the apostle Paul thinks, 'I could easily correct that man's mistakes; I could tell him that the Lord created all things in six days, and rested on the seventh, and show him in the Book of Genesis the inspired account of the creation.' 'But, no,' he says to himself, 'I have a more important message than that to deliver.' Still, he must have felt as if he would have liked to set him right; for, you know, when you hear a man uttering a gross falsehood, you feel as if you would like to do battle with him. But instead of that, the apostle just thinks, 'It is not my business to set the people right about their theory of the creation of the world. All that I have to do is to know nothing but Jesus Christ, and him crucified.'[3]

How then should ordinary ministers and preachers respond in the present climate of unbelief and scepticism supported by evolution?

CHS True ministers are sons of thunder, and the voice of God in Christ Jesus is full of majesty. Thus we have God's works and God's

Word joined together: let no man put them asunder by a false idea that theology and science can by any possibility oppose each other.4

You obviously feel that the preachers ought to be more resolute in their stand.

CHS Under the Jewish law no man who had a squint was allowed to be a priest (Leviticus 21:17–23). I wish they would make a similar law with regard to spiritual sight in preachers nowadays, because some of them are sadly cross-eyed as they look to Moses and to Darwin; to revelation and to speculation!5

How then should pastors and preachers respond to evolutionism and other doctrines that infiltrate the churches?

CHS The apostle, in his day, had to contend against those who ran away from the simplicity of the gospel into all manner of fables and inventions. Such, in our day, are the doctrine of evolution, the doctrine of the universal fatherhood of God, the doctrine that everyone will be saved, and all sorts of fables and falsehoods which men have invented.6

What about those who have already become theistic evolutionists and have tried to import evolution into the Bible's message?

CHS The Holy Spirit minister chooses Jesus for his main theme. He does not speak about modern science and the ways of twisting Scripture into agreement with it.7

Do you think it is only the desire to be well thought of that drives preachers to compromise their position on the early chapters of Genesis?

CHS Today there is the temptation of love for intellectual novelty. Instead of the old, old gospel, and the old, old Book, we are to place science, which is generally conjecture, in the place of revelation; and the thoughts of men cover and bury the sublime thoughts of God. Ministers and churches are deluded and led astray by these temptations. As for me, I purpose in my heart not to defile myself with this portion of the king's meat, nor with the wine which he drank.[8]

I know the apostle Paul said that some people ease up in case they should suffer persecution for the sake of the gospel. Perhaps it is this that so unsettles some preachers and believers.

CHS Some do have this fear. They say, 'Here is a new danger, how are we to meet it?' It was anxiously asked, a few years ago, 'How are we to meet these discoveries of geology?' Yet we hardly ever hear about them now, or, if we do, we do not trouble about them. Then Dr Colenso[9] had made calculations which were very terrifying to timid folk, and Huxley tried to prove that we had descended or ascended from monkeys; but who cares about their theories now? Yet I have met with nervous people who greatly feared the fury of this tyrant named Science, which was supposedly going to utterly destroy us, but what has it ever done successfully against the truth?[10]

I have heard some preachers say that though the Bible is without error in matters of faith, there may be errors about history and geography. How do you respond to that?

CHS We must never allow into our minds a suspicion of the incorrectness of the Word of God in any matter whatever, as though the Lord himself could err. We will not have it that God, in his holy Book, makes mistakes about matters of history, or of science, any more than he does upon the great truths of salvation. If the Lord be God, he must be infallible. If he can be shown to be in error in the little respects of human history and science, he cannot be trusted in the greater matters.[11]

But, do you not at least admit that the Bible is not a science book?

CHS That is very true, but the Bible never makes a mistake in its science, and I would rather agree with the old writers, who held that the Bible contained all science, than I would go with those who blasphemously pretend to correct the Holy Spirit, and to set him right upon geology, and whatever else. In the long run, it shall be proved that the old Book beats all the scientists, and when they have made some wonderful discovery, it will turn out that it was all recorded here long before.[12]

But I have read books by Christian authors that say Genesis 1 is poetic prose and therefore is not a literal, historic account of creation. They call it a 'myth', meaning a religious story intended to convey deeper truths. What do you make of that?

CHS This is, no doubt, a literal and accurate account of God's first day's work in the creation of the world.[13]

What about those who say it is poetry not history?

CHS It is a very great sin on the part of Christian soldiers, to make false alarms to discourage and dispirit their fellow-soldiers. There are some professors who seem to delight to tell us of a new discovery in science which is supposed to destroy our faith. Science makes a wonderful discovery, and straightaway we are expected to doubt what is plainly revealed in the Word of God. Considering that so-called 'science' is continually changing, and that it seems to be the rule for scientific men to contradict all who have gone before them, and that, if you take up a book upon almost any science, you will find that it largely consists of repudiations of all former theories, we can afford to wait until they have made up their minds as to what science really is. At any event, we have no cause to be distressed concerning science, so let no Christian man's heart fail him, and let him not raise any alarm in the camp of Christ.[14]

But sometimes those who hold to long ages and macro-evolution, even where they try to put a First Cause in the picture, bring evidences or arguments that we just cannot answer. How should we respond?

CHS At times you and I are assailed as to our faith in the Bible, by people who say, 'How do you make that out? It is in the Scriptures, certainly, but how do you reconcile it with science?' Let your reply be, 'We no longer live in the region of argument as to the Word of the Lord; but we dwell in the realm of faith. We are not squabblers, itching to prove our superiority in reasoning, but we are children of light, worshipping our God by bowing our whole minds to the obedience of faith. We would be humble, and learn to believe what we cannot altogether comprehend. It is our ambition to be great believers, rather than great thinkers; to be child-like in faith, rather than intellectually "clever". We are sure that God is true! Like Abraham, we do not stagger at the Word of God, because it seems improbable or apparently impossible. What the Lord has spoken he is able to make good; and none of his words shall fall to the ground.'[15]

I accept that trying to win the argument is not the way to win the battle, but often we are expected to have an answer ready for the questions we are asked about science and the Bible.

CHS There are those who, while not exposed to persecution, *do* have to stand against the assaults of unbelief. That which believers in past ages have accepted as truth, is not believed in many places today; and so it comes to pass that one brings to us a bit of sceptical science which he has picked up from Huxley or Tyndall; another comes with a criticism that he has found in one of the modern theologians, who are the devil's instruments for spreading unbelief; and a third appears with a vile blasphemy from one of the coarser assailants of religion, and each one demands an immediate answer to his quibble, or his difficulty. Do they really expect that we are to answer, on the spur of the moment, every objection that they are pleased to raise? I confess that I do not believe that one human brain is capable of answering every objection that another human brain could raise against the most obvious truth in the world. I specially advise that you do not try to answer fault-finders; but if you do, mind that faith is your weapon. If you take the wooden sword of your own reasoning, you may easily be beaten. Speak as the Lord guides you. Fix in your mind, 'This is God's Book. This is his infallible revelation, and I believe it against every argument that can possibly be urged against it. Let God be true, but every man a liar.' This will be sure defensive ground; but if you get off that rock, you will soon find yourself sinking or staggering. For an offensive weapon, take 'the sword of the Spirit, which is the word of God'; and if this does not serve your turn, nothing will. Have a thorough, entire, and childlike faith in the revelation of the Most High, and you will be made strong in those mental conflicts for which in yourself you are so weak.[16]

Wouldn't it be a good thing if we could gather an army of university professors and world-class scientists to answer the objections raised by evolutionists, theistic or atheistic? Perhaps then we would see more people coming to Christ as well.

CHS You do not find the Lord calling in the pomp and prestige of worldly men to promote his kingdom, or see him arguing with philosophers that they might sanction his teaching. Christian ministers do this, and I am sorry they do. I see them taking their places in the Hall of Science to debate with the men of boastful wisdom; they claim to have won the argument there, and I will not question their claim, but I fear they will never win spiritual triumphs in this way. They answer one set of arguments, and another set is invented the next day. The task is endless. To answer the allegations of infidelity is as fruitless as reasoning with the waves of the sea, so far as soul-saving is concerned. This is not the way of quickening, converting, and sanctifying the souls of men.[17]

I suppose you are right. But wouldn't it be nice if the atheists were at least answered and silenced once and for all?

CHS I am not trying to make my beliefs appear philosophical or probable: far from it! We do not ask that men should say, 'That can be supported by science.' Let the scientific men keep to their own sphere, and we will keep to ours. The doctrine we teach neither assails human science, nor fears it, nor flatters it, nor asks its aid.[18]

But if we could prove that the Bible is true, that miracles did and do happen, and that the greatest miracle of all is a fact of history, surely you believe that even the most hardened sceptic would give way to fact.

CHS Can't you see that if this very day a man should rise from his tomb, and come here to affirm the truth of the gospel, the unbelieving world would be no more near believing than it is now?[19]

Surely not!

CHS Think about it! Here comes Mr Infidel Critic. He denies the evidences of the Bible; evidences which so clearly prove its authenticity, that we are obliged to believe him to be either blasphemous or senseless, and we leave him his choice between the two. But he dares to deny the truth of Holy Scripture, and will have it that all the miracles by which it is attested are untrue and false. Do you think that one who had risen from the dead would persuade such a man to believe? [20]

Surely the evidence of a man rising from the dead would be overwhelming? They couldn't deny it!

CHS No! I see the critical blasphemer already armed for his prey. Listen to him, 'I am not quite sure that you ever were dead, sir, you profess to be risen from the dead; I do not believe you. You say you have been dead, and have gone to heaven; my dear man, you were in a trance. You must bring proof from the parish register that you were dead.' The proof is brought that he was dead. 'Well, now you must prove that you were buried.' It is proved that he was buried. 'That is very good. Now I want you to prove that you are the identical man that was buried.' 'Well I know I am. I tell you as an honest man I have been to heaven, and I have come back again.' 'Well then,' says the infidel, 'it is not consistent with reason. It is ridiculous to suppose that a man who was dead and buried could ever come to life again, and so I don't believe you.' And certainly, if the wonder were done in some far-off land, and only reported to the rest of the world, I suppose that the whole sceptical world would exclaim, 'Simple childish tales. Sensible men do not believe them.' Although a churchyard should start into life, and stand up before the sceptic who denies the truth of Christianity, I declare I do not believe there would be enough evidence in all the churchyards in the world to convince him. Infidelity would still cry for something more. Prove a point to an unbeliever, and he wants it proved again; let it be as clear as noonday to him from the testimony of many witnesses, and still he does not believe it. In fact, he does believe it; but he pretends not to do so.[21]

I once heard of someone saying, 'My mind is made up, don't bother me with facts.' So, although the evidence exists, the foundation of faith is a trust in the unassailable and permanent trustworthiness of the holy Scriptures.

CHS The rock of God's Word does not shift, like the quicksand of modern scientific theology. One said to his minister, 'My dear sir, surely you ought to adjust your beliefs to the progress of science.' 'Yes,' said he, 'but I have not had time to do it today, for I have not yet read the morning papers.' One would have need to read the morning papers and take in every new edition to know where scientific theology now stands; for it is always chopping and changing. The only thing that is certain about the false science of this age is that it will be soon disproved. Great scientists live by killing those who went before them. They know nothing for certain, except that their predecessors were wrong. Even in one short life we have seen system after system rise and perish. We cannot adapt our religious belief to that which is more changing than the moon.[22]

We seem though to be fighting this battle on every side. There are both atheistic scientists and modern theologians. They are united in both opposing the idea of the truth of the Bible. How can we win?

CHS Suppose that all these men, who will not believe, should get together to proclaim new views in order to upset the gospel. You see, up to the present time, they never have agreed. One wing of Satan's army of doubters always destroys the other. Just now the great scientists say to the modern theologians, and say to them very properly, 'If there is no serpent, and no Eve, and no Adam, and no flood, and no Noah, and no Abraham—as you tell us now that all this is a myth—then your whole Book is a lie.' I am very much obliged to those who talk in this way to the disciples of higher criticism. They thought that they were going to have all the scientists on their side, to join them in attacking the ancient orthodoxies, but there is a split in the enemy's camp![23]

I see the truth of what you say. If I were an atheist I would laugh in the face of those who tried to use evolution and fit it in with the Bible account. I would think them foolish, dishonest or deliberately cowardly and treacherous. Even with their contradictions and divisions, atheistic and theistic evolutionists view themselves as having one common enemy against which they are both implacably opposed—biblical creationism. What is to be our strategy against this coalition of disparate views?

CHS He whom God sends cares nothing at all about human wisdom, so as to fawn upon it and flatter it; for he knows that 'the world by wisdom did not know God' (1 Corinthians 1:21); and that human wisdom is only another name for human folly. All the learned men and the philosophers are simply those who profess themselves to be wise, but are not. Yet we face false science with 'the foolishness of preaching', and set up the cross in the teeth of this intellectual self-sufficiency.

Are we to make no allowances for what is called the 'honest agnostic', or the 'thinking man'? Couldn't we appeal to them by having debates and discussions, so that people can think the issue out for themselves? I don't mean to undermine preaching, but you must be aware that straightforward preaching from the Bible isn't exactly popular.

CHS People want 'thinking' nowadays, so it is said, and the working man will go where science is deified and profound 'thought' is enshrined. I have noticed that as a general rule wherever the new 'thinking' drives out the old gospel there are more spiders than people, but where there is the simple preaching of Jesus Christ, the place is crowded to the doors. If it is foolish to preach up atonement by blood, we will be fools; and if it is madness to stick to the old truth, just as Paul delivered it, in all its simplicity, without any refinement, or improvement, I mean to stick to it, even if I am pilloried as being incapable of progressing with the age, because I am persuaded that this 'foolishness of preaching' is a divine ordinance, and that the cross of Christ which stumbles many, and is ridiculed by many more, is still the power of God and the wisdom of God.[24]

So how do preachers lose confidence, not only in preaching, but also in the message itself? They adopt false interpretations of Genesis that eventually lead them into all kinds of difficulties with their doctrine of the Bible, man, sin, the origin of death, and even the Person and work of Christ. How does it happen?

CHS Have you never noticed a constitutional tendency in some who profess faith to stumble, and get lame? If there is a swamp, they fall into it; if there is a thicket, they get entangled by it; if there is an error, they run into it. They are good people, and they believe in Jesus; but, somehow or other, they do not see things clearly. Such people go off at a tangent if anybody makes noise enough to attract their attention. Let some theologian discover a new doctrine, and they are on its track at once, never thinking where it will lead them. Some would-be philosopher suggests a fresh theory, which clashes with the Word of God, and their eager appetite is whetted, and they leave the old fields of truth to wander in the barren wastes of science falsely so-called. There is, sadly, in our congregations, no lack of these good, thoughtless people, lame and limping in their walk, troubled with scepticism, and plagued with curiosity.[25]

But what about those who preach evolution mixed in with their gospel and do not believe in the inerrancy of Scripture?

CHS Whenever men pretend great reverence for Jesus, and then seek, by their erroneous teaching, or their science falsely so-called, to overthrow his gospel, they are base hypocrites.[26]

But surely those preachers and believers, who hold the halfway house between creation and evolution, called theistic evolution, should, at least, win the respect and attention of atheistic scientists?

CHS On the contrary! We never dreamed that we should feel grateful to Professor Huxley for an opinion on theology; but we confess our obligations to him for a comment in the 'Agnostic Annual', where he writes, 'On the whole, the "bosh" of heterodoxy is more offensive to me than that of orthodoxy; because heterodoxy professes to be guided by reason and science, and orthodoxy does not.' Let those who imagine that they are pleasing great scientists, by perpetually bowing and scraping to them, see how their lowly adorations are received. Sensible men know how to value the compliments of those who can cut and shape their creed according to the last new fad of scientific theorists. I am not surprised that the poor, unreasonable, orthodox believer should be less offensive to any kind of honest man than the creature who knows nothing whatever of 'science', and yet has the word for ever on his tongue.[27]

I hope you don't think this a spurious question, but is there anything that gospel preachers might actually learn from these scientists?

CHS It was observed by a very excellent critic not long ago, that if you were to hear thirteen lectures on astronomy or geology, you might get a pretty good idea of what the science was, and the theory of the person who gave the lectures; but if you were to hear thirteen hundred sermons from some ministers, you would not know at all what they were preaching about or what their doctrinal sentiments were. It ought not to be so. Is not this the reason why all sorts of errors have such a foothold, because our people as a whole do not know what they believe?[28]

Apart from learning to be more theologically substantial and definite in preaching, is there anything else that is commendable among scientists from which preachers could learn?

CHS Think of the earnestness of men of the world in their callings and pursuits. How men will wear themselves out in seeking the secular objects on which their hearts are set! To what sacrifices will they expose themselves! The advocates of science completely shame the followers of religion. They have penetrated into the densest swamps, defying fever and death; they have lost themselves among the wildest savages. Science daily increases her martyrology, but where do we find ours? Where is the chivalry of Christians? Where are the heroes of the cross? In former times followers of Christ did not count their lives dear for his sake, but now we hug ourselves in ease, and attempt little for the Lord. The world has warm followers and devoted friends, but Jesus is attended by a lukewarm band of men who are more likely to sleep at Gethsemane's gates than to watch with him for a single hour. 'Oh Lord of love, forgive our sin, and from this good hour teach us how to live.'[29]

There certainly is a need for the Lord's people, and especially his ministers, to take serving Christ in their generation more seriously.

CHS Yes, when a man wants to make money, see how he rises early, and sits up late, and eats the bread of carefulness! It is wonderful what ingenuity men put forth to get a fortune. They will go to India and sweat under the burning sky, and brave the fever there. Why, there are thousands of England's sons who do this every year. See how at the North Pole bold and brave men have sacrificed their lives to force a passage. Men have been willing in scientific experiments to sacrifice social comforts, risk their health and forfeit their lives. It seems to me that everybody is enthusiastic except Christians, and men can get their blood hot on any subject except religion. Look at the devil's advocates, how they cross sea and land to make one disciple.[30]

But when friends or family see a person zealous for Christ they immediately think the person is fanatical or demented if he or she is devoted to the study of the Bible or spends hours in trying to spread the gospel.

CHS Many are scientific zealots; they will sacrifice health in sitting over mixtures of detrimental drugs to examine chemical combinations; or they will pass through feverish countries among savage men to discover the source of a river, or measure the height of a mountain. We can easily find business zealots: their shop windows scarcely need shutters, for business is never over. They steal Sunday for their bookkeeping; they hurry to be rich; they plunge into this speculation and the other; they often bring their bodies to sickness and their minds to madness in their zeal for riches. You do not find that the world cries out against zeal in business, in science and in politics. Men can admire it there, but the moment you bring it into the court of the Lord's house, then immediately they hold up their hands with astonishment, for men cannot endure that we should make eternal things real and spend our strength for them; they would have us reserve our energies for the matters in which they take so deep an interest. I would not condemn the use of zeal in the common affairs of life, for zeal is essential to success; we only wish that Christians would take the lead from worldly men and be half as earnest and ambitious to maintain and increase the kingdom of their Lord and Master, as some men are after petty trifles.[31]

Let's get back to the main subject of creation and evolution. Do you think it is worth the effort in trying to understand the issues it raises?

CHS The Bible speaks of profane and idle babblings and contradictions of what is falsely called 'science' (1 Timothy 6:20). We are overdone with these canker-worms at this hour. You can go and interfere in all the controversies of the day if you like, but beware of the consequences. I like that expression of Mr Wesley's preachers, when they were asked to interfere in this or that political struggle, they replied, 'Our work is to win souls, and we give ourselves to it.' Oh that churches would listen to this just now! They are going in for amusements, and the church is vying with the theatre. Oh that we would lay hold on eternal life, and seek the salvation of men. Eternal life in our churches would soon cast out the rubbish which is now defiling them. Jesus in the churches would purify the temple of the puppets, as once he cleansed it of the traders. We need to receive this conviction again: that our one great business here below is to lay hold on eternal life, first making our own calling and election sure, and then seeking to bring others to Christ. Other questions compared with this are trivial debates.[32]

If we take your advice and put our whole confidence only in the gospel and the preaching of the cross rather than discussion, and entertaining people to attract them to our meetings, we are likely to be laughed out of court.

CHS The men of Noah's generation mocked him. He preached to them; but many would not hear him, for they thought him mad. Those who did listen said to each other, 'He is building a boat on dry land: is he sane? We are scientific, and therefore we know how absurd his preaching is; for no one ever heard of the world being drowned by a flood.' They called his warning 'an old wives' fable'. They called him 'an old fossil'. He was undoubtedly the frequent object of sarcasm. I cannot reproduce the letters that were written about the sturdy patriarch, nor can I recount the spiteful things which were said by the gossips; but I have no doubt they were very clever, and very sarcastic. Those productions of genius are all forgotten now; but Noah is remembered still. For all the scorning he received he went on obeying his God: he stuck to the lines on which God had placed him, and he could not be turned to the right hand or to the left, because he had a real faith in God.[33]

The man in the street thinks of Noah's Ark as a fairy tale. He pictures a small boat with elephants and giraffes with their heads sticking out of a play boat. Such images make the whole story a laughingstock.

CHS Let me direct your attention to the size of the ark; it may comfort you. It was immense. It is an old objection of unbelievers that there was not room enough in it for all kinds of creatures that lived on the face of the earth; but we know, on divine authority, that if there had not been enough room for all the different kinds of creatures which were then alive, they would have been drowned, so room enough was found for them all. This is not very logical, you say, but it is conclusive enough for anyone who believes in revelation. There really is no reason for anyone to make the objection, since the most eminent calculators have proved conclusively that the vessel called the ark was of immense size, and was able, not merely to hold all the creatures, but all the provisions they would require for the year during which it floated on the water.[34]

I suppose, anyway, his preaching was proved right, even though he stood alone in his generation.

CHS Yes, and I also would rather speak five words out of this Book than fifty thousand words of the philosophers. I had rather be a fool with God than be a wise man with the sagest scientist, for 'the foolishness of God is wiser than men; and the weakness of God is stronger than men' (1 Corinthians 1:25).[35]

You answer in a way that makes me ashamed I ever asked the question! So, how can we, who are preachers and not scientists, be so confident in our preaching about creation and how it all happened? Should we not be humble and hesitant about these things? Please take time to answer more fully.

CHS We are invited to go away from the old-fashioned belief of our forefathers because of the supposed discoveries of science. What is science? It is the method by which man tries to conceal his ignorance. It should not be so, but it is. You are not to be dogmatic in theology, my brethren, it is wicked; but for scientific men it is the correct thing. You are never to assert anything strongly, but scientists may boldly assert what they cannot prove, and may demand a faith far more credulous than any we possess. You and I are to take our Bibles and shape and mould our belief according to the ever-shifting teachings of so-called scientific men. This is folly! Why, the march of science, falsely so called, through the world may be traced by its exploded fallacies and abandoned theories.

I have said before that former explorers once adored are now ridiculed; the continual wrecking of false hypotheses is a matter of universal notoriety. You can tell where the learned have made camp by the debris left behind of suppositions and theories as plentiful as broken bottles. As the quack doctors, which ruled the world of medicine in one age are the scorn of the next, so it has been, and so it will be, with your atheistic know-alls and pretenders to science. They say they remind us of 'facts'. They should be ashamed to use the word. Wonderful 'facts', made to order, and twisted to their will to overthrow the actual facts which the pen of God himself has recorded! Let me quote one from *Is the Book Wrong?* by Mr Hely Smith: 'For example, deep down in the alluvial deposits in the delta of the Nile were found certain fragments of pottery. Pottery, of course, implies potters, but these deposits of mud, Sir Charles Lyell decreed, must have taken 18,000 years to accumulate, therefore there must have been men following on the occupations of civilized life at least 7,000 years before the creation of man as recorded in Scripture. What clearer proof could be wanted that the Book was wrong? For who would presume to suspect Sir C. Lyell of making a mistake in his work? A mistake, however, he had made, for in the same deposits of mud, at the same depth in which this "pre-Adamite pottery" was discovered, there also turned up a brick bearing the stamp of Mohammed!' (AD 570–632). If their cause had not been so weak, what was the necessity for trying to strengthen and supplement it by presenting the public with false statements?[36]

Do you believe that we need a real return to the unreserved and

wholehearted confidence in the preaching of the gospel that has been so obviously blessed by the Lord in other times?

CHS When the gospel was preached in that royal style it mightily prevailed, and annihilated opposition. Faultfinders came, of course. 'What does this babbler want to say?' (Acts 17:18) was a common question; but the heralds of the cross made short work of them, for they simply went on declaring the glorious gospel. Their one word was, 'This is from God: if you believe it you shall be saved, if you reject it you shall be damned.' They made no bones about it, but spoke like men who believed in their message, and judged that it left unbelievers without excuse. They never altered their doctrine or softened the penalty of refusing it. Like fire among stubble, the gospel consumed all before it when it was preached as God's revelation. It does not spread today with equal rapidity because many of its teachers have adopted what they fancy are wiser methods: they have become less certain and more indifferent. They reason and argue where they should proclaim and assert. Some preachers rake up all the nonsense that any scientific or unscientific man likes to bring forward, and spend half their time in trying to answer it.[37]

But is there no value in answering these issues?

CHS What can be the use of untying the knots tied by sceptics? They only tie more. If we get back again to the old platform, and speak as from God, he will surely honour his own Word. The preacher should either speak in God's name or hold his tongue. My brother, if the Lord has not sent you with a message, go to bed, to school, or mind your farm; for what does it matter what you have to say from yourself? Alas for the weakness of human wit and the fallacy of mortal reasoning! But if we deliver what God declares, we have a simple task, and one which must lead to grand results, for the Lord has said, 'My word shall not return unto me void.'[38]

Thank you. We will take another break before talking about those who may disagree.

Notes

1 'The People's Christ', *NPSP* 11. Psalm 89:19.

2 'So It Is', *MTP* 2175. Job 5:27.

3 'Christ Crucified', *MTP* 2673. 1 Corinthians 2:2.

4 *The Treasury of David*, Volume 1. Psalm 29.

5 'Eyes Right', *MTP* 2058. Proverbs 4:25.

6 'The Whole Gospel in a Single Verse', *MTP* 2300. 1 Timothy 1:15.

7 'Additions to the Church', *MTP* 1167. Acts 2:47.

8 'Dare To Be a Daniel', *MTP* 2291. Daniel 1:8.

9 The Bishop of Natal from 1853 until his death, despite an attempt to have him deposed in 1863. It was while writing *Pentateuch and Book of Joshua Critically Examined* that he cast doubt on the authorship and accuracy of those Bible books, including the statistics they contain, for instance, concerning the numbers involved in the Exodus from Egypt.

10 'Needless Fears', *MTP* 3098. Isaiah 2:12–13.

11 'The Obedience of Faith', *MTP* 2195. Hebrews 11:8.

12 'A Strange Yet Gracious Choice', *MTP* 2600. Psalm 135:4.

13 'Light Natural and Spiritual', *MTP* 660. Genesis 1:1–5.

14 'Discipline in Christ's Army', *MTP* 3188. Joshua 1:11.

15 'Noah's Faith, Fear, Obedience and Salvation', *MTP* 2147. Hebrews 11:7.

16 'The Best Strengthening Medicine', *MTP* 2209. Hebrews 11:34.

17 'The Gentleness of Jesus', *MTP* 1147. Matthew 12:19–21.

18 'The Resurrection Credible', *MTP* 1067. Acts 26:8.

19 'A Preacher from the Dead', *NPSP* 143. Luke 16:31.

20 *Ibid.*

21 *Ibid.*

22 'The Infallibility of Scripture', *MTP* 2013. Isaiah 1:20.

23 'God Justified, though Man Believes Not', *MTP* 2255. Romans 3:3–4.

24 'Soul Saving Our One Business', *MTP* 1507. 1 Corinthians 9:22.

25 'Lame Sheep', *MTP* 2854. Hebrews 12:13.

26 'A Popular Exposition to the Gospel According to Matthew', Matthew 22.18. (This is his commentary on Matthew's Gospel, in its cover sheet known as: *The Gospel of the Kingdom, A Popular Exposition to the Gospel according to Matthew, by Charles Haddon Spurgeon, with Introductory Note by Mrs C. H. Spurgeon.* The quotation given in the document is from the exposition of Matthew 22:18 in that commentary.

27 *The Sword and the Trowel,* 1884. Notes.

28 'Salvation Altogether by Grace', *MTP* 703. 2 Timothy 1:9.

29 'My Prayer', *MTP* 1072. Psalm 109:37.

30 'The Arrows of the Lord's Deliverance', *MTP* 569. 2 Kings 13:19.

31 'Zealots', *MTP* 639. Luke 6:15.

32 'Eternal Life within Present Grasp', *MTP* 1946. 1 Timothy 6:19.

33 'Noah's Faith, Fear, Obedience and Salvation', *op. cit.*

34 'The Parable of the Ark', *MTP* 3042. Genesis 7:15.

35 'Come from the Four Winds, O Breath!' *MTP* 2246. Ezekiel 37:9.

36 'The Evils of the Present Age, and How to Meet Them', *The Sword and The Trowel,* 1877.

37 'The True Gospel No Hidden Gospel', *MTP* 1663. 2 Corinthians 4:3–4.

38 *Ibid.*

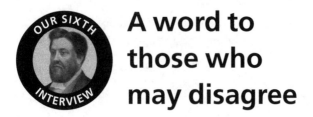

A word to those who may disagree

In this last interview may we first discuss those preachers and pastors who say they have a regard for the Scripture and believe in a creator, but mix evolution into the Genesis record. Some of these preachers are held in the highest evangelical esteem.

CHS God has allowed to come into his vineyard a number of religious teachers who are not rendering to him due honour. Those religious teachers I am referring to are not teaching the gospel as it is delivered in holy Scripture, but they are adapting it to the age, and to the scientific knowledge of the period.[1]

I know some, for whom this has been the beginning of a slippery slope leading them into all kinds of errors, and even scandalous behaviour that they then also excuse, saying they can justify it from the Bible.

CHS It is evidently true that men do not long hold to theism pure and simple. If our scientific men get away from Christ, the incarnate God, before long they drift away from God altogether. They begin to slide down the mountain when they quit the incarnate Deity, and there is no other foothold to stop them.[2]

Where do you think this mixing of evolutionary science and a belief in an error-strewn Scripture will eventually lead?

CHS We need somebody to take these various preached ideas, put them into a cauldron, boil them down, and see what is produced. Some of you may have seen in the newspapers a short time ago an article with regard to the moral state of Germany. The writer, himself a German, says that the scepticism of the professed preachers of the Word, the continual doubts which have been suggested by scientific men and more especially by professedly religious men as to revelation, have now produced in Germany the most frightful consequences. The picture which he gives makes us fear that our Germanic friends are treading on a volcano which may explode beneath their feet. The authority of the government has been used so severely that men are burdened under it and, meanwhile, the authority of God has been put so much out of the question that the basis of society is undermined. The French revolution at the end of the eighteenth century also remains in history as an enduring warning of the dreadful effects of philosophy when it has created a nation of unbelievers. May the same not happen here, but the party of 'modern thought' seems resolved on repeating the experiment. So greatly is the just severity of God ignored, and so small an evil is sin made out to be, that if men were to be doers of what has been taught from certain professedly Christian pulpits, anarchy would be the result.3

Moving on from supposed Christians who hold to evolution, atheists often speak of religion, and particularly of Christianity, as if it is the cause of so much of the grief in the world. How do you respond to them?

CHS Where are the triumphs of infidelity in rescuing men from sin? Where are the trophies of philosophy in conquering human pride? Will you bring us prostitutes that have been made pure; thieves that have been reclaimed; angry men, of bear-like temper, who have become harmless as lambs, through scientific lectures?[4]

That is a powerful argument. One thing I have noticed is that atheists are so certain they have found the truth, and yet it seems a message of despair to confidently affirm, 'We have come from nowhere. We are here for no purpose. We are going nowhere.' They have nothing worth saying, yet they often rage at Christians trying to do good.

CHS If someone says, 'I do not believe in Christ,' then what do you believe in? For, whatever you believe in, try to use it for the good of your fellow men. I would like to see you sending city missionaries from street to street to preach what you do believe in. Let them do something more than find fault. Some are so fond of pulling down. Why not try a little building up? Come then! You atheists say that we Christians are doing no good. Just try your own hand at it. Go to the dying: go to the sick; take them bottles of your philosophy, and comfort them with the elixir of scientific doubt. Go ahead! If somebody says that the current system of medicine is faulty, I reply—Very well, have you found the right medicine? 'Yes.' Then distribute it, train physicians, and build hospitals. Get to work at it. Now, you that do not believe in God or Christ, send your own missionaries abroad. Enlighten the heathen by telling them that there is no God, no sin, no hell, no heaven, no soul, no anything. Go into primitive cultures, and win them from their deadly superstitions by the doctrines of science. Go ahead. If you have a gospel do not hide it. What? You have no zeal in that direction. But why not? There is no particular use in it, is there? It's not worth spending your money on. Miserable comforters! Wretched physicians that cannot heal! But now, if you want to know whether there is power in the cross, ask a city missionary to let you go with him for a day. Choose the right man, and go and see for yourself. He will show you what the doctrine of the cross can do in comforting, sobering, cheering and elevating. 'I do not believe it,' says one. No one said you did. I will, however, venture to observe that, 'The proof of the pudding is in the eating,'—a good old English proverb. Here is a ship filling with water, and you do not believe in pumps. Very well. I am going on pumping. You are anxious to discuss. Discuss away, but meanwhile I pump. Let every Christian man here make practical use of the cross of Christ, and keep on at it, and if men will not even take the trouble to enquire what are its results, their disbelief is irrational and inexcusable, and they must take the consequences.5

Despite having a message without hope, they have a very condescending spirit to believers—as if they pity our simplicity and ignorance.

CHS 'No fool like a learned fool' is a true proverb. When a man has done with God, he has done with his manhood, and has fallen below the level of the ox and the ass, for 'the ox knows its owner, and the ass its master's crib' (Isaiah 1:3). Instead of being humbled in the presence of scientific infidels, we ought to pity them; they look down on us, but we have far more cause to look down on them.[6]

Do you think this pride in their own intellect explains why so few of these people ever accept the good news that God has provided a crucified and risen Saviour for sinners? I recall that Wesley wrote that even in revival, few important, elderly or wealthy people came to faith in Christ.

CHS Some abhor the cross of Christ because the gospel is so simple. They belong to a club, and they take a magazine for intellectuals. They do not know very much about any one thing, yet they know a little about a great many things. They get a smattering of various kinds of knowledge, and think they are wonderfully clever. You cannot expect that they would have anything to do with the gospel that would suit a servant girl. The religion that fits Jack and Tom is not grand enough for them. Why, they actually had a distant relative who was connected with a baronet, so of course we cannot expect such gentlemen as they are, to be saved simply by believing on the Lord Jesus Christ. The gospel is too plain, too easy, for them. Would they like to have it made difficult, so that all the poor ignorant people in the world might perish just to please them? Let me remind you that Sir Isaac Newton, one of the greatest of all human minds, gloried in the gospel of Jesus Christ, and felt it all too great for him. Such a truly scientific man as Faraday bowed meekly before the divine Saviour, and looked up and found everything in him. Yet some foolish people think they know better than the eternal God, so they hate the cross. Self-conceit is the reason of much of the opposition of men to Christ.[7]

But there are those who say they just cannot believe what they cannot see. One atheist I heard said that if he died and found out there was a God, his defence would be, 'Not enough evidence!'

CHS When scientists tell us that they cannot see God I am amazed. It is impossible not to see him. I cannot pry with scalpel into the anatomy of the human frame, yet when I simply look upon the skin of the human face I see the handiwork of God. I cannot dig into the lower strata of the earth and disentomb the fossil and decode its stone-preserved memorial, yet to me rock, and clay, and sand, and relic of the past, bear the sure hieroglyph of God. I cannot inform you of all the intricate details of insect life, or speak about the secrets of botany, yet bees bring me honeyed thoughts of God, and flowers breathe the perfume of his love. 'Where is God?' You ought to ask rather, 'Where is he not?' I am no fool, for this Bible in my hand, the best authority, declares that he is the fool who says in his heart, 'There is no God' (Psalm 14:1). Yes, the whole earth is full of the glory of Christ. Above the earth it is seen in every cloud. Above the cloud every star shines out concerning him. What poor blind eyes that cannot see what is evidently set forth everywhere. Poor ears which cannot hear, when earth and sea, and heaven and hell, are all echoing to the tread of the omnipotent Christ of God.[8]

But have you noticed how they make a substitute for God? Atheists talk of nature as if it is a living thing. They give nature the attributes of deity!

CHS In former times there were those who traced everything they saw to 'chance'. That malformed deity has been laid aside, and on its pedestal men have set up another idol called 'Nature'. They attribute everything that is great and wonderful to 'Nature'. They forever talk of 'the beauties of Nature', 'the grandeur of Nature', 'the laws of Nature'; but God is spoken of as if he were not alive. What are laws of nature but the ordinary ways in which God works? I know of no other definition of them. But these people attribute to them a sort of power apart from the presence of the Creator. I heard a street preacher say that we could not do better on Sunday than go abroad and worship Nature. There was nothing that was so refining and elevating to the mind as Nature. Nature did everything. A Christian man in the crowd ventured to ask, 'What is Nature?' And the gentleman said, 'Well, Nature—well—it is Nature. Don't you know what it is? It is Nature.' No further definition was forthcoming. I fear the term is only useful as enabling men to talk of creation without being compelled to mention the Creator. Man does not like to think of his God. He wants to get away into a far country, away from God his Father, and he will adopt any sort of phrase which will help him clear his language of all trace of God. He longs to have a convenient wall built up between himself and God. The heathen often attributed their prosperity to 'fortune', some of them talked of 'chance', others speak of 'fate'. Anything is to man's taste rather than blessing the great Father, and adoring the one God. If they prospered, they were 'lucky'; this was instead of gratitude to God. We have those now who thank their lucky stars. They know God exists, but do not honour him as God.[9]

How then should those who are serious students of the natural world approach their search for the meaning of life, or perhaps even their search after the knowledge of God the Creator?

CHS Nature demands attention, hard and persevering, from those who would be true scientists. The Word of God certainly deserves as reverent an investigation as his Works. Why should not the Scriptures be studied thoroughly? Even as mere literature they will well reward careful study. It is the part of a wise man calmly and earnestly to search those famous writings which are prized by so many masterminds. The voice which cried to Augustine, 'Take! Read!'[10] was no foolish advice. To take up and read a great and good book cannot be to our detriment.[11]

I know that in this search to know God, the first great word is 'repent'. It calls us to a thorough change of mind. How does this apply to those who are absorbed in the area of thought we have been discussing—Darwinian theory? After all, it may be very costly to accept that everything one has thought, taught and believed for years is completely wrong?

CHS You cannot have Jesus, and have the world too. You must break with sin to be joined to Jesus. You must come away from the licentious world, the fashionable world, the scientific world, and from the (so-called) religious world. If you become a Christian, you must quit old habits, old motives, old ambitions, old pleasures, old boasts, old modes of thought. All things must become new. You must leave the things you have loved, and seek many of those things you have so far despised.[12]

The second great word in the gospel is 'believe'. Again, what does it mean to those from a scientific background to believe in Christ?

CHS Every boy at school has to exercise faith. His schoolmaster teaches him geography, and instructs him as to the form of the earth, and the existence of certain great cities and empires. The boy does not know that these things are true, except that he believes his teacher, and the books put into his hands. That is what you will have to do with Christ if you are to be saved—you must just know because he tells you, and believe because he assures you it is even so, and trust yourself with him because he promises you that salvation will be the result. Almost all that you and I know has come to us by faith. A scientific discovery has been made, and we are sure of it. On what ground do we believe it? On the authority of certain well-known men of learning, whose reputation is established. We have never made or seen their experiments, but we believe their witness. You are to do the same with regard to Christ. Because he teaches you certain truths you are to be his disciple, and believe his words, and trust yourself with him. He is infinitely superior to you, and presents himself to your confidence as your Master and Lord. If you will receive him and his words you shall be saved.[13]

If you could sit down with one of these men or women and speak earnestly to them, what would you say to them?

CHS I would speak in this way. 'Though you began by being an opposer, may you end by being a friend!' There was a club of gentlemen, meeting together to discuss literary and scientific subjects, and, after a long discussion, they agreed to burn the Bible, and one of them was about to do it. They had selected about the boldest of them to do it but, as he was going to take it to the fire, his hand trembled, and, laying it down, he turned round, and said, 'I think we had better not burn this Book till we find a better one.' And I think we may say of those who, in these days, are trying to kick against Scripture, they had better let it alone until they find a better one.[14]

It is not just that they do not see. I suspect for many it is that they refuse to see. I know people personally who have made it their life's goal to disprove the gospel. Their opposition is solely to the Christian faith, nothing else. Have you met people like that?

CHS Yes, there are some who exert their utmost skill for nothing else but to discover discrepancies in the gospel narratives, or to conjure up differences between their supposed scientific discoveries and the declarations of the Word of God. Often they have torn their own hands in weaving crowns of thorns for Christ. I fear some of them will have to lie on a bed of thorns when they come to die, as the result of their displays of scientific research after briers with which to afflict the Lover of mankind. They should beware of lying on worse than thorns for ever, when Christ shall come to judge them and condemn them and cast them into the lake of fire for all their impieties concerning him.[15]

Let me thank you for these interviews and ask you to draw to a close with comments to those who either find evolution attractive and persuasive, or, at least, do not find the biblical doctrine acceptable to them.

CHS If you think rightly, you will submit to think as God thinks. If your thoughts are what they should be, they will not contradict God's thoughts, for he knows more than you, and knows better than you. Is the Infinite, the Eternal, to be judged by man's judgement? Is he to be analysed in the chemist's laboratory? Are his thoughts to be ridiculed because they are contrary to the reigning philosophy, which is probably no more true than the many other forms of human ignorance which have previously come and gone in the centuries of the past? Will not this present dream of mortal wisdom melt like a mist before the sun of gospel truth? Is God's great system of salvation and providence to be called to the bar of the scientists, who can do no more than dote after the manner of their predecessors? These wise men so despise the teaching of the Lord that one would think they were a committee of doctors examining a maniac. Let us abhor the presumption of scepticism, and let us be wise enough to know our folly; rational enough to feel that God is to be obeyed, and not questioned; and that his revelation is to be believed, and not criticized. Though we think crookedly, God's thoughts are upright; though we think grovellingly, God thinks sublimely: though we think in a finite and erroneous way, God thinks infinitely and infallibly; and it is ours continually to correct our thoughts by the infallible Word, so that our minds are kept in harmony with the sure utterances of the Holy Spirit.[16]

In closing, how can we pray for a generation that seems so deluded by evolution?

CHS Pray to the Lord in these terms. 'Take away, we pray, the itching for new doctrine, the longing for what is thought to be scientific and wise above what is written, and may your church come to her moorings, may she cast anchor in the truth of God and abide there; and if it be your will may we live to see brighter and better times.'[17]

Notes

1 'The Pleading of the Last Messenger', *MTP* 1951. Mark 12:6–9.

2 'Love's Law and Life', *MTP* 1932. John 14:15.

3 'Two Sorts of Hearers', *MTP* 1467. James 1:22–25.

4 'Three Crosses', *MTP* 1447. Galatians 6:14.

5 'Is It Nothing to You?' *MTP* 1620. Lamentations 1:12.

6 *The Treasury of David*. Psalm 94:8.

7 'The Enemies of the Cross of Christ', *MTP* 2553. Philippians 3:18–19.

8 'Israel and Britain: a Note of Warning', *MTP* 1844. John 12:37–41.

9 'Knowledge, Worship, Gratitude', *MTP* 1763. Romans 1:20–21.

10 Spurgeon originally used the Latin.

11 'The Clue of the Maze: Let Us Live.'

12 'No Compromise', *MTP* 2047. Genesis 24:5–8.

13 'Faith: What Is It? How Can It Be Obtained?' *MTP* 1609. Ephesians 2:8. (This is repeated almost exactly in 'All of Grace'.)

14 'Unmitigated Prosperity', *MTP* 2963. Isaiah 53:10.

15 'The Crown of Thorns', *MTP* 1168. Matthew 27:29.

16 'God's Thoughts and Ways far above Ours', *MTP* 1387. Isaiah 55:8–9.

17 'On Holy Ground', Prayer 12, *C. H. Spurgeon's Prayers*.

What if Spurgeon is mistaken about the age of the Universe?

What I want to ask now is quite sensitive because you have said that before the creation week there may have been a long period when chaos reigned, until the earth had cooled down and was then formed and filled for habitation by man. I understand fully that you believe this arranging, furnishing and filling of the world was accomplished in six twenty-four hour days. However, evangelicals now understand that Archbishop Usher largely got it right, and those who try to fit a gap in between Genesis 1:1 and the following verses are mistaken in their interpretation of the Bible text as a whole. Some of your statements may therefore be misunderstandings of both the facts of creation and the meaning of the text of the Bible. How do you respond to this?

CHS The Lord's church may do wrong, his ministers may be mistaken, but Christ himself can never be in error.[1]

So, as I understand it, you are saying there are no mistakes in the Bible account.

CHS I say without hesitation that there is no mistake whatever in the original holy Scriptures from beginning to end. There are mistakes of translation; for translations are not inspired, but the historical facts are correct. There is not an error anywhere in them. The words come from him who can make no mistake, and has no wish to deceive his creatures.[2]

I suppose we all misunderstand parts of the Bible.

CHS Half of the heresy in the church of God is not wilful error, but those which spring of not knowing the truth, not searching the Scriptures with a teachable heart and not submitting the mind to the light of the Holy Spirit. We should, as a rule, treat heresy as ignorance to be enlightened rather than a crime to be condemned. That is, except when it becomes wilful perversity, when the mind is greedy after new ideas, or puffed up with self-confidence: then other treatment may become painfully necessary.[3]

What if you have made a mistake, as I believe you have in this 'gap theory'?

CHS If in anything I have erred, it has been an error of judgement; I may have been mistaken, but so far as I have understood the truth, I can say that no fear of public or private opinion has ever turned me aside from what I hold to be the truth of my Lord and Master.[4]

But, in your case, people may follow not only your correct views, but your misunderstandings. They may say, 'If my pastor can believe it, so can I.'

CHS Never say, 'My beloved pastor went there, and therefore I may go there.' No, but say, 'Even our minister fell into that error, and therefore I will keep as far from it as I can, for if the teacher slips, the disciple may easily fall too.'[5]

What should people, who respect your judgement, do then?

CHS Go home and search. I have told you what I believe to be true. If it is not true, detect the error by reading your Bibles for yourselves, and searching out the matter.[6]

What advice is there for those who accept a thing because C. H. Spurgeon said it?

CHS I may teach errors through lack of carefulness or through the weakness of my own mind. In the greatest preacher or teacher that ever lived there was some degree of error. Therefore you should always bring what I say to the Bible, because the Holy Spirit never teaches error.[7]

I was quite reluctant to raise this issue, especially as you are so particular to affirm the inerrancy, infallibility and sufficiency of Scripture, but you seem to have a very humble spirit and sensitive conscience concerning the possibility that you may have taught any error.

CHS Error is always injurious, however innocent may be its shape, and however poetic may be the terms in which it is expressed. May God ensure we have nothing to do with sin or error, for these things cannot be good; they must be evil.[8]

Do you not think it diminishes our usefulness if we teach a mix of error and truth?

CHS No doubt there is a great deal of work which God owns although all in it is not truth. God prospered the work of Whitefield and Wesley; but did that prove the truth of all that Whitefield or Wesley preached? No, but it proved that both of them had a measure of truth in their preaching, and God blessed that measure of truth; but God would not establish anything that they taught in error. It may last for a while, and some of it has lasted, I am afraid, much longer than is good for us; but it will have to go sooner or later. What a mercy it is, if I do some mischief when I am trying to do my Master's work, and the good work I do lasts, but the bad I do, forgiven by his infinite mercy, shall soon, by his great wisdom, be swept away![9]

Do you really believe that about your own misunderstanding of Scripture?

CHS May anything that I hold of error be blasted with the breath of the Almighty, and anything that is held that is error in any other church be withered and dried up as the grass before the mower's scythe! May it fall and utterly perish. But every truth everywhere, and every truth-holding man, may they be immortal. And grace anywhere, grace everywhere, wherever it is; if it is the grace of God, may it go on to grow stronger and stronger, and may it conquer.[10]

I suppose a clear conscience in the integrity of teaching honestly what you believe to be the correct interpretation of Genesis 1–11 is a comfort in itself.

CHS Yes! It is a sweet thing to be able to say, 'I may have been mistaken, but I have honestly sought to know the mind of God, and with earnest dependence upon the Holy Spirit I have desired to accept his teaching; and, as far as I have understood it, I have followed it, regardless of the consequences of doing so, knowing that it must always be safe to follow where the Spirit leads the way.'[11]

I also find it difficult to frame my doctrines only from the Bible. There are so many cultural or other pressures that subtly influence how I interpret it.

CHS To get rid of old prejudices and preconceived notions is a very hard struggle. It is well said, that those few words, 'I am mistaken,' are the hardest in all the English language to pronounce, and after having done so, it is difficult to wipe away the slime which an old serpentine error has left on the heart. Better for us not to have known at all than to have known the wrong thing. If I had been left alone to form my notion of God, entirely from Holy Scripture, I feel, that with the assistance of his Holy Spirit it would have been far more easy for me to understand what he is, and how he governs the world, than to learn after my mind had become perverted by the opinions of others.[12]

But it isn't easy to do that, is it?

CHS When we come to the Bible, it must be honestly and humbly, with this feeling, 'I desire now to unlearn the most precious doctrine or practice I have ever learned if the Lord will show me that it is inconsistent with his will; and I desire to learn that truth which will bring me most into derision, or that duty which will submit me to the greatest inconvenience, if it is his will, for I am his servant.' I think we shall all get closer together, if, in the Spirit of God, we begin reading our Bibles in this way.[13]

Thank you for so helpfully disclosing your heart in relation to any errors you may hold.

Notes

1 'The Best of Masters', *NPSP* 247. John 14:27.

2 'The Bible Tried and Proved', *MTP* 2084. Psalm 12:6.

3 'Our Urgent Need of the Holy Spirit', *MTP* 1332. Romans 15:13,19.

4 'The Minister's Farewell', *NPSP* 289. Acts 20:26–27.

5 'Strong Faith', *MTP* 1367. Romans 4:20.

6 'David's Dying Song', *NPSP* 19. 2 Samuel 23:5.

7 'The Teaching of the Holy Ghost', *NPSP* 315. John 14:26.

8 'Two Good Things', *MTP* 1629. Psalm 119:71.

9 'Established Work', *MTP* 3142. Psalm 90:17.

10 '15: A Comprehensive Prayer', Able to the Uttermost: twenty Gospel sermons selected from unpublished manuscripts.

11 'Honour for Honour', *MTP* 2906. 1 Samuel 2:30.

12 'The Prodigal's Return', *NPSP* 176. Luke 15:20.

13 'A Call to Holy Living', *MTP* 1029. Matthew 5:47.